Positively ADD

*Real Success Stories
to Inspire Your Dreams*

POSITIVELY ADD

Real Success Stories
to Inspire Your Dreams

CATHERINE A. CORMAN
AND
EDWARD M. HALLOWELL, MD

Walker & Company New York

Seelan Manickam as an adult, photo courtesy Steven Emery © 1999
Sharon Wohlmuth as an adult, photo courtesy Michael Ahearn
Harbhajan Singh Khalsa as an adult, photo courtesy Catherine A. Corman
Richard Joseph Zienowicz, MD, FACS, as an adult, photo courtesy Catherine A. Corman
Oman Frame as an adult, photo courtesy Edward M. Hallowell, MD
Clarence Page as a child, photo courtesy Olan Mills

Text copyright © 2006 by Catherine A. Corman and Edward M. Hallowell, MD

First published in the United States of America in 2006 by
Walker Publishing Company, Inc.
Distributed to the trade by Holtzbrinck Publishers

For information about permission to reproduce selections from
this book, write to Permissions, Walker & Company,
104 Fifth Avenue, New York, New York 10011.

Library of Congress Cataloging-in-Publication Data

Corman, Catherine A.
Positively ADD : real success stories to inspire your dreams / Catherine A. Corman and
Edward M. Hallowell.
p. cm.
Includes bibliographical references.
ISBN-10: 0-8027-8988-9 • ISBN-13: 978-0-8027-8988-4 (hardcover)
1. Attention-deficit-disordered adults—Interviews. I. Hallowell, Edward M. II. Title.
RC394.A85C67 2006   616.85'89—dc22   2005037184

Book design by Nicole Gastonguay

Visit Walker & Company's Web site at www.walkeryoungreaders.com

Printed in the U.S.A.

2 4 6 8 10 9 7 5 3 1

TABLE OF CONTENTS

Acknowledgments and a Dedication vii

A Note to Young People viii

A Note to Parents and Other Adults xi

PROFILES

Chester James Carville Jr., *Political Strategist* 1

Scott Eyre, *Relief Pitcher, Chicago Cubs*....................................7

Carolyn O'Neal, *Retired School Principal*....................................15

David Neeleman, *Founder, Chairman,*
and CEO, JetBlue Airlines 25

Karl V. Euler V, *Police Officer* 33

Heather Long, *Graduate Student,*
Rhodes Scholar 43

Devin M. Barclay, *Professional Soccer Player,*
Columbus Crew 54

Margaret Turano, *Director, Marketing*
Communications, Amicas 63

Richard Joseph Zienowicz, MD, FACS, *Plastic*
and Reconstructive Surgeon 72

Seelan Paramanandam Manickam, *Musician* 80

Sharon Wohlmuth, *Photographer* 91

Harbhajan Singh Khalsa, *Yogic Healer* 101

Oman Frame, *Teacher* 109

Clyde B. Anderson, *Chairman, Books-A-Million* 119

Jon Bonnell, *Chef* 127

Linda Pinney, *Entrepreneur, Chief Business Officer, Asteres* 138

Clarence Page, *Journalist*, Chicago Tribune 148

Resources 157

Common Questions and Answers About ADD 159

Acknowledgments and a Dedication

We would like to thank all of the courageous individuals whose stories are in this book. They spoke graciously and humorously with us about living well with ADD. Without their honesty and insights, we would have no book at all.

Thank you to Jill Kneerim, our agent and brilliant matchmaker, for having the ingenuity to help forge our partnership. Thanks also to Emily Easton at Walker & Company, who understood our dream and helped to make it real. Without the practical assistance of Margaret Myers and Lisa Douglis, this book would have been much harder to produce.

We dedicate *Positively ADD* to our families. We are grateful, especially, for the support of our spouses, Mark Penzel and Sue Hallowell. We offer this book to the next generation: Lily, Max, Sam, Lucy, Jack, and Tucker. Accept these stories as a reminder that we believe in you and celebrate the special qualities in each of you. Persist, dear ones, and don't forget that a challenge is nothing more than a chance to try.

Catherine A. Corman
Brookline, MA
Edward M. Hallowell, MD
Sudbury, MA

A Note to Young People
by Edward M. Hallowell, MD

We wrote this book for you. Both Cathy and I have children with Attention Deficit Disorder, or ADD, and I have ADD myself, so we care a great deal about this syndrome and the people who have it. We want you to know the truth about life with ADD.

Here's the truth:

- ADD does not have to keep you from achieving your dreams. Indeed, it can help you do exactly that.
- To achieve your dreams, you have to find out what you're good at. Then you have to practice.

The stories in this book will show you how *real* people with ADD have figured out what they are good at.

ADD is different in every person, and no one should think of himself or herself as being just ADD. You're much, much bigger than ADD!

ADD typically differs in girls and boys, although, as you'll see in this book, there are exceptions. Most often, girls with ADD are not noisy, hyperactive, or disruptive. Usually, they are dreamy and easily distracted, but they aren't rambunctious the way boys with ADD tend to be. Boys tend to be the ones who have trouble sitting still or doing what they're told to do, which gets them in trouble. For this reason, boys are twice as likely to be diagnosed with ADD than girls; but whether it's because it's more noticeable in hyper boys or truly more common is not entirely clear. Boys and girls like this don't mean to cause trouble, but they are just so full of energy, it is hard for them to settle down.

Whether or not you have the kind of ADD that includes extra energy, if you have ADD, I can guarantee that you have special talents. As you grow up, you need to discover those talents and develop them. This can be a lot of fun. If you focus on developing your talents, you will get better and better at what you're working on.

You'll need to be careful not to get sidetracked spending too much time trying to get good at the things that you like the least and find the hardest. Of course, you're going to *have* to do some of these things, perhaps with a tutor or organizational coach during or after school. That may not be your idea of fun, but it's important to do, all the same. You'll be building mental muscles and good habits that will strengthen you for the rest of your life. *You can do it.* Never forget that.

Meantime, don't lose sight of the big picture. Be sure your parents, teachers, guardians, and coaches let you spend a big chunk of your time trying to strengthen talents and explore what you enjoy. As you'll learn reading this book, by developing those passions and talents, you'll be taking the first, most important steps toward creating a great life with ADD.

It doesn't matter what your favorite activities are. They could be playing the violin, baking fancy cakes from scratch, chasing a ball on a soccer field, auditioning for the school musical, organizing fund-raising drives, competing on the debate team, or designing and sewing clothes. This past summer, my sixteen-year-old daughter, who has ADD, made a dress. She wants to be a fashion designer. Her mother and I aren't concerned that fashion design is not a subject in school. We want to help her find ways to develop her own special talents.

Having ADD is a gift, but it can be a hard gift to unwrap. Once you've opened the package, you will see that ADD is actually a beautiful present. The best way to unwrap it is to keep getting better at all you do, especially what you love to do. You will need to ask for help along the way. You will need to be persistent—refusing to give up—because you will get frustrated at times. You will sometimes wish you didn't have ADD, but as you learn to take advantage of the good side of it, you may surprise yourself. You may find that, like all the people in this book, you are glad you have it.

If you hear people say bad things about ADD, ignore them because they don't know what they're talking about. Some people just like to say bad things. That's their problem. Don't make it yours. Albert Einstein and Thomas Edison had ADD, as well as the interesting, happy, successful people in this book.

Each story in this book will provide you with a new example of how a person has developed his or her special talents. As you read about these people you will discover that life with ADD does not have to be bad. Indeed, it can be all that you ever dreamed life could be. No doubt, the going will get tough at times, but with hard work, determination, and help from other people, you will survive and thrive.

For proof, read on.

A Note to Parents and Other Adults
by Edward M. Hallowell, MD

A little boy sits in my office, his head down, eyes hidden from view, as his mom looks anxiously from him to me and back to him. "Why won't you go back to school?" she asks her son.

"Because school stinks," he replies.

"Maybe if we tried, we could find a way to make it stink less?" I volunteer.

"No. No. No," he says emphatically. "I've tried whatever you're going to say. I've tried everything. You don't get it. The problem is, I'm stupid." At that, he pounds his head with his fist. "I am a broken part. I should have been thrown out. I hate who I am." Even though this twelve-year-old boy is highly intelligent and gifted in many ways, he has concluded with absolute certainty that he ought to be tossed in the garbage.

His mom looks at me with desperate eyes. As a child psychiatrist in practice for over twenty years, I have come to know those eyes well. They are familiar to me from talking with many moms and dads who have watched their children suffer simply because they learn differently and do not fit into the mold that most schools try to force on them.

Later, after the boy has left the room, this mom will ask me the searing questions every parent whose child learns differently eventually asks: "What is going to become of my son in this world? Is there any hope? Will anyone besides me ever see how talented and special he is?"

I will listen as the mother speaks, feeling her agony as well as her devotion to her son, and I will feel the upsurge of awe I always feel in the presence of these wonderful, heaven-sent mothers. Along with the fathers, they bravely battle on, trying whatever they can to protect their children from the psychological battering that schools often unconsciously administer. I am heartened when I hear about schools trying to nurture the special talents that these parents, and sometimes *only* these parents, know their children possess. Oh, if only I heard about such schools more often.

No matter how much I would like, I will not be able to make everything all right for this mother and others like her right then and there. But I will do what I can. I will tell this mother what for the past twenty years I have been telling mothers, fathers, teachers, brothers, sisters, grandparents, coaches, and anyone else who will listen: "Not only can your son survive, he can thrive. The talents you and I know he has will emerge and carry him to great places. He will make a terrific life for himself. But this will take patience, persistence, imagination, and a lot of work on your part and on his."

And then, as in most of these conversations, this mom will ask me how I know. I can see in her eyes that she is weary, tired of the cycles of hope and disappointment she's lived through for years.

I tell her I know because I've seen it before. I know because I know what she's made of, and I know what her son's got going for him. "I don't think this world can stop either one of you," I tell her, "as much as it will try."

A glimmer of hope shines through those sad eyes. "Tell me," she says. "Tell me about when you've seen it before."

At that point, I will wish I could give her the book you now have in your hands.

I will wish I could give her this collection of true stories about men and women from many different backgrounds and many different places, all of whom struggled to overcome the obstacles that having ADD put in their way.

I will wish I could do more than reassure this mother and encourage her but also actually *prove* to her, through factual accounts lifted from the lives of real people, that a great life is *realistically* possible, no matter what kind of mind you happen to be born with.

When Cathy Corman proposed the idea for this book and asked me to work with her, I jumped at the chance. As a father and as a doctor, I knew how much young people, parents, and teachers needed to read about positive examples of life with ADD. Now, in collaboration with the generous men and women who told us their stories, we have the book that holds the proof of how good life with ADD can be. At last, I can hand over this book and say, "Just read this. You can see for yourself."

The people in these stories have had to deal with one special kind of mind, the kind characterized by what we misleadingly call attention deficit disorder, or ADD. About fifteen million children and adults—at least 5 percent of the U.S. population—have the syndrome called ADD. It appears in every ethnicity, race, religion, and region. It is a worldwide phenomenon. International studies in India, Indonesia, Italy, and Germany estimate that the incidence of ADD is even higher in those places than it is in the United States. ADD is usually inherited, as you will see in this book. Some children seem to grow out of ADD, but most go on to become adults with ADD. There are two main types of ADD. One produces quiet, distractible daydreamers. The other produces distractible, impulsive, hyperactive daydreamers. Having ADD has nothing to do with intelligence or IQ, although it appears to correlate with heightened creativity and imagination.

The weaknesses associated with ADD are not reflected in the label. In fact, the label "Attention Deficit Disorder" misses the essence of what is going on in ADD. People with ADD do not suffer from a lack of attention. Instead, their hypersensitive attention wanders, and often to interesting places. At times, people with ADD can pay rapt attention, but they do not always pay attention to what they are supposed to. They may have difficulty gathering their observations and ideas in an orderly fashion so that others can understand them. This can cause trouble.

In the years to come, we will know much more about what is going on with ADD. At present, the model we work with emphasizes what is wrong, damaged, disordered, and in need of correction. The positives associated with ADD have received little notice.

What a mistake.

If you tell people of any age, and most certainly children, only what is wrong, damaged, disordered, and in need of correction in their lives, you create a more severe problem than the one you are trying to fix. Indeed, I have observed that the most damaging learning disorder is not ADD but shame and fear, the feelings that develop in people when their noses are rubbed in their shortcomings every day.

While it is necessary to deal with the problems that come with ADD, you will learn from the stories in this book that growth begins with positive energy. When people find something they can do well or when they find a person who believes in them, then, and only then, are they likely to develop their talents and strengths and overcome the challenges that come with ADD.

People with ADD also wrestle with getting organized, being on time, making plans, following through to the end of tasks, keeping up with ongoing projects, taking care of details, and prioritizing what needs to be done next. These so-called executive functions can wax and wane in people with ADD, leading to a pattern of underachievement. Many people see this behavior as evidence of laziness, lack of interest, or lack of drive and commitment. Most of the time, nothing could be further from the truth. People with ADD are typically ferociously tenacious. They are not lazy—but they can get lost. And they can agonize as they try to find not the easy way out in life but the right way in.

As you read the stories in this book you will see what an ordeal life with ADD can be. You will see how discouraging it can be to try and to fail over and over again. You will see how tempting it can be just to give up—both for the person who has ADD and for the people who are trying to help. The people who have shared their personal struggles with you show that with effort, with help, and with determination, there is good reason to believe that the ordeal will come to an end and open onto a very satisfying life.

Those people we profiled explained repeatedly the significance of being able to name and claim their differences. Most found their diagnoses profoundly liberating, feeling, at last, that they could come to terms with their struggles. With their diagnoses also came an ability to develop strategies to compensate for the hard things and make the most of special talents.

The people we have profiled are proud of who they are. They say they would not give up their ADD even if they could. Though they all use different words and relate different stories, all of them have found that the single most important trick to living a great life with ADD is to learn how to promote the gifts and contain the problems. Go with the good, they say, and try not to let the problems trip you up too often. Rather than focusing on what's wrong with people who have ADD, they say, look carefully to find what's right and draw that out.

Cathy and I both have children who have ADD, and I have ADD myself, so we are especially interested in what happens to such children when they grow up. We know firsthand that life with ADD isn't easy. For people who have ADD, and for those who raise them, teach them, coach them, employ them, befriend them, or marry them, life can be especially difficult. But there can be happy endings. We want our children to read about people who have ADD and have made their lives into something good, who enjoy who they are and enjoy the lives they are living. We want our children—and other children, not to mention other adults—to read true stories that might inspire them and give them a dose of the most powerful medicine we know: hope. Hope summons a positive energy that can propel a person from a life of frustration to one of mastery and joy.

We believe in the power of biography to teach and to inspire. We looked for real people who have wrestled with ADD and won the match. To be included in this book, they had to have ADD as diagnosed by a reliable professional, and they had to be successful and happy. We defined "successful" as having met their major goals in life so far, and we defined "happy" as having the feeling that their lives were going well.

The gallery of people you will find in this book shows what tremendous variety goes into the diagnosis of ADD. It also demonstrates that the paths a person with ADD can take to find success and happiness are many and varied. These stories prove that having ADD does not lead to misery and failure or close off any career or dream. Never again should any guidance counselor or teacher in any school, or any admissions officer at any university or professional school, or *any person anywhere* tell parents, or worse, tell children and young adults that because they have ADD, they shouldn't bother to pursue what they love or really want to do.

These stories show that while people with ADD can

achieve great success and find true happiness, they rarely do so by conventional routes. They often need more time than those without ADD to figure things out and to thrive. False starts and true blunders are par for the course.

Consequently, if you are raising young people with ADD, you'll need an extra reserve of patience and understanding. You have to think creatively when there seem to be more loose ends than happy endings. Structure must always be a big part of strategies and solutions. Aimless wandering, while romantic, is to be avoided for those who have ADD, who need to stay safe while they search for their true callings.

Consider several examples from this book. When Richard Joseph Zienowicz forgot to take the admission test for medical school, he didn't drop out of sight. He got a job working in a psychiatric hospital. The structure of a job helped prevent him from getting into trouble and also steered him in a positive direction. When James Carville flunked out of college, he didn't drift around. Instead, he enlisted in the military for a few years, which gave him time to figure out how he wanted to get through college and into law school. When David Neeleman left college, he didn't just veg out, doing nothing, sitting around his parents' house. Just the opposite. He worked long, arduous hours developing his creative ideas in travel and aviation. Now he heads an airline.

It's easy to feel sorry for kids with ADD, but pity won't do anyone any good. Without structure, kids with ADD can quickly lose hope and get into serious trouble before they find their way. Don't let them give up or tune out. Their route to success may be roundabout, and the timetable may, like so much in the world of ADD, be utterly unpredictable. When will the train pull into the station? You may not know, but rest assured, it *will* arrive in its own remarkable way.

How a person feels about having ADD largely determines the outcome of that person's life. Therefore, it is crucial, from as early as possible, that children with ADD feel good about who they are. Lives with ADD can be happy, successful, vibrant, and fulfilling—as long as shame and fear do not prevent people with ADD from taking on challenges.

So take heart. Not only is there hope, there is also factual evidence that good times await.

CHESTER JAMES CARVILLE JR.

Political Strategist

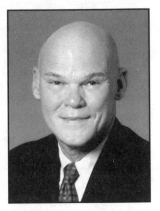

Failure is just a part of life. Go out and fall flat on your face about a hundred times before you expect to get things right.

Date of Birth: October 25, 1944
Washington, DC

AT SIXTY-ONE, JAMES CARVILLE CAN'T SIT STILL. He never could. "I am *not* a lingerer," he says proudly in an energetic Southern drawl. "Restaurants *love* me. I have a drink, I eat, I get up, I tip big, and I don't hold up people. At home, I'm the first one up from the dinner table. My mother used to say, 'You're like a toaster. You just pop up all the time.'"

A brilliant strategist who has helped politicians in America and abroad—including former president Bill Clinton and former Israeli prime minister Ehud Barak—get elected, James jokes that he is a "pamphleteer and raconteur," a person who knows how to get the word out and tell good stories. Author of six books, he currently cohosts a TV talk show, writes, and is helping to produce a new movie version of the novel *All the King's Men*, a story about the spectacular rise and fall of a Southern politician.

1

Early Years of the Ragin' Cajun

Nicknamed "The Ragin' Cajun" on account of his fiery character and Acadian roots, James always knew he was different. He knew it as a kid, and he's known it as an adult. He describes himself as impulsive and impatient, eager for stimulation and interaction with others. The nuns at Catholic school made him sit in the front of the classroom, where they could keep an eye on him. If he misbehaved, they'd swat him with a piece of wood. Writing and taking tests were especially tough. "Give me a number two pencil and a bunch of questions—well, you'll just terrify me," he says.

Classes didn't get any easier after high school. James couldn't pass Spanish and flunked out of college at Louisiana State University (LSU) in 1966. Then he spent two years in the marines, getting what he describes as "a kick in the butt" that gave him the sense to get serious about school. He taught high school during the day and finished his degree in night school at LSU. He wasn't sure what to do next. "People said, 'You're a good talker. You oughta be a lawyer,'" James remembers.

A Lawyer?

At first, James liked this idea. As a white person growing up in Carville, Louisiana (a tiny town in the rural South named after his grandfather), James saw African Americans suffering from poverty and racial discrimination. He wondered if he could use the law to help people. Most white people in the 1950s and 1960s where James's family lived believed that if African Americans couldn't go to good schools, get good jobs, or vote, then it was how God wanted things. James did not agree. "I grew up in a place where there was no issue other than race," he says. "I had a different opinion on the defining issue of the day."

James earned his law degree in 1973 from LSU. He tried working as a lawyer in Baton Rouge, Louisiana, until 1979. Despite his hopes of using the law to change things, James realized he hated working as an attorney. "I looked up one day, and I thought, 'If I had to hire a lawyer, I wouldn't hire *me*,'" he says, laughing. "There never was anybody more ill-suited to the law than I was. I mean, title searches, that kind of stuff . . . yuck!"

Still passionate about making America a fairer place for African Americans, James started volunteering on political campaigns, helping to elect candidates who shared his views. "It dawned on me," he says, "you know, something I'm really good at is *this*." James left the law and began to work full-time on campaigns.

Campaigns:
Something I'm Really Good At

By running political campaigns, James brought all of his interests and abilities together, and his weaknesses hardly mattered at all—in fact, they were strengths. "I was very lucky that I was able to find something I really liked and cared about, i.e., politics, that I could do," he says. At last, he says, his "skills were valuable to someone."

Political campaigns are a great fit for many people with ADD, James says. Campaign managers have to be great storytellers, knowing how to get a message from a candidate's mouth to voters' ears. They've got to explain very quickly what voters need to understand. "Speed matters, and concision matters," he says. "These are two of the things we ADD people have in spades." There are never "typical days," he says, so it's impossible to get bored. "Ten things happen at once," James notes. "The schedule comes out, the candidate will say something wrong, there are TV people coming, you get polling results, you put out a questionnaire, and somebody's got to talk to you *right now!*"

Campaigns have clear beginnings and ends, which, James says, is terrific for people who have trouble completing long assignments. "A campaign gives you a project, and it ends on a certain day, with results that are certain," he says. Best of all, he says, is that you don't have to wait around forever to find out how you've done: "You either win or you lose." And by the way, James says, "I *like* winning!"

ADD in the Family

James doesn't think he could have won as many times as he has without ADD. "I don't think I could have done what I did in my life without having the ability to concentrate in short bursts," he says. "If I look back, I think that having ADD is actually a positive thing." It was only fairly recently that James knew how to explain the things that are different about him in terms of ADD. His wife took him to a doctor when he was in his midfifties. ADD was on their minds because their eldest daughter had been diagnosed with ADD.

In the doctor's office, after the doctor had finished talking, James told him he didn't want to try medications. "I said, 'I don't really want to change. I don't really want to be anybody else. I'm not dissatisfied with the way I am. In fact, I am quite satisfied.'" Granted, like most people with ADD, James is disorganized, and he says he constantly loses things. "If I put a total value on everything I've lost in my life—shoot!" he exclaims. But, he says, he also has more fun and is more creative than most people.

You Just Gotta Suck It Up

With this kind of perspective, he doesn't worry too much about children who have ADD—his kids or other people's kids. "I am not in the least bit disturbed," he says, about his daughter's ADD. "I know she's going to be able to see things and experience things that other people aren't going to be able to do." Sure, he wishes his daughter didn't have to suffer through things in school that don't come easily—like math tests—but, "You just gotta suck it up. There's no getting around it. I wish there was." For him, athletics always helped him focus, so he played team sports in school. Now he runs for thirty to forty-five minutes every afternoon. "It can really help me concentrate. I get my best thoughts when I'm running."

James wants kids to know that success doesn't have to come quickly or easily. "Failure is just a part of life," he says. "Go out and fall flat on your face about a hundred times" before you expect to get things right. That's what happened to him. It took a long time for him to find politics. He was a "late bloomer," he says, not hitting his stride in a career until he was in his late thirties, and not marrying until he was in his late forties. Sometimes, he says, you've got to fail frequently until you're in a position to succeed.

I Woulda Hired Me

Now known all over the world for his ability to help political candidates get elected and lead well, James routinely gets asked to give lectures and talk about current events. Success, he says, has been a wonderful surprise. "I've always been proud of what I did. Proud of the way I earned a living. It's just an awful good hand to get dealt in life that you get to do something you really wanted to do, to be successful at it, to be happy in it. Do I think I've done some good in the world? I like to think so."

"There was a time in my life," James remembers, "when I realized that if I had to hire a political campaign manager, I woulda hired *me*. That's the best feeling you can have."

Scott Eyre

Relief Pitcher, Chicago Cubs

*When people put
me down, it made
me work harder.*

Date of Birth: May 30, 1972
Bradenton, Florida

STANDING ON THE MOUND, STARING DOWN at Manny
Ramirez or Carlos Beltran or some other hungry hitter who
wants to turn on his next pitch and drive it out of the park,
Scott Eyre doesn't think about anything but the moment. He
is where he has wanted to be ever since he was a child. But he
is not thinking about that when he's pitching. In fact, he is
not *thinking* at all, in the usual sense of the word. He is one
with his task. Not able even to describe what it's like himself,
he is in a place where exertion, cleverness, and guts combine
in a cauldron of such fiery focus that everything else in the
world melts away.

Scott holds the ball that was rubbed in dried mud before
the game by the dutiful umpire who is now Scott's judge. He
stares in, looks for the catcher's sign, and prepares to do battle
with the hitter. He is totally present, every bit of his mental

energy centered on the game: his pitch choice, where the catcher is setting up, what the runners on first and second are doing as they take leads off their bases. Of all the roles in Major League Baseball, none requires more focus and more grace under pressure than that of the relief pitcher. When he comes into the game, his team is usually in trouble. His job is to walk in calmly and try to turn things around. This is what Scott Eyre does for a living. It is one of the most difficult jobs in the world. He handles trouble. Big-league trouble.

Focus!

"It's kind of funny that my job is based on focusing and being able to come in with a couple of runners on base and get them out," Scott says. "And remember, I am supposed to get them out day in and day out."

It's funny because Scott has a job that requires exceptional focus *and* he has ADD, a disorder of which lack of mental focus is commonly thought to be a main symptom. And not only does he do the job, he does it at the highest level possible: he's playing Major League Baseball.

Little League

Getting to that level took incredible talent, courage, and work. From the beginning, the odds were against him. Scott's mom and dad got divorced when he was eight years old. That meant his mother had to raise, and earn the money to support, Scott and his four siblings by herself. Being the oldest, Scott tried to help, but it was his mom who really shouldered the load.

"Mom worked all kinds of jobs," Scott says. "She did some child care at our house, out of our home. She worked at a hotel cleaning up. She'd vacuum the hallways and clean the lounge and do whatever she could do. She got a job at Kmart, and she worked in the women's and kids' departments for almost ten years."

Now that Scott is a big-league pitcher, he makes plenty of money; but when he was a child, he had very little. "For the better part of my youth," he relates, "we had a two-bedroom house and one bathroom. We were pretty close together."

Minor League

Although school was difficult for Scott, he did well enough to be allowed to play ball. He had trouble sitting still and paying attention in class. He says he did his best because he knew that if he didn't pass his classes, he wouldn't have been allowed to play baseball, which he loved with a passion. He managed to get through high school, graduated, and headed off to Southern Idaho Junior College, hoping to get a degree in *anything* in case he couldn't fulfill his dream of becoming a professional ballplayer.

After Scott's first year in Idaho, he got drafted by the Texas Rangers. He turned down the offer, since he didn't think it was good enough to make it worth leaving college.

When the Rangers came back with a better offer, he decided to accept, since the pay he would earn would help his family.

"It was $35,000," Scott states. "Not much by today's standards. I was a ninth-round draft pick. Guys in the ninth round nowadays get $75,000 to $80,000. But I took it and went to the Instructional League in Port Charlotte, Florida. The pay was so low that in the off-season, I got jobs working at a Toys "R" Us and ushering at a movie theater."

His rise to "The Show," as minor leaguers call the major leagues, was tough. Earning low pay, having to work extra jobs to get by, having no job security, trying to keep his dream alive, Scott lived the hard life of a minor leaguer. There was no glamor whatsoever. Just long bus rides to small cities for the next game, lots of chewing gum, card games, and cheap meals each and every day. No headlines. No spots on ESPN. Just a young man trying to keep his hope alive.

Major League

Scott was tenacious. He was determined to do all he could to reach his goal. Then disaster hit. Scott blew out his elbow during a game in August 1994. He'd suffered a devastating, career-ending injury before his career had even really started. Many men would have packed it in at that point, maybe gone back to school or just taken whatever job they could find. But not Scott. He spent the entire year working with trainers in Florida to get better. He didn't want to walk away from the game he loved to play without giving it all he had.

At that time, he met a woman who helped him. "I met her

at a bar during that rehab year," Scott says. "I went out one night, and this pretty girl caught my eye. When it came to girls back then, I was fairly quiet; so I asked one of my buddies on the team to go over and ask her if she wanted to meet us somewhere. I went out and met her at another bar. We just started talking, and we talked all night. I asked her for her phone number and said, 'Hey, I'll call you tomorrow.' To this day I think she thought, 'Oh, he'll never call.' But I did. We went out. The rest is history. We've been married for eight years. She is awesome. She's everything I could want in a wife. I know everyone says this, but she is truly my best friend."

Scott finished his rehab in great condition. His hard work paid off. The Chicago White Sox signed Scott to pitch. The team gave him a start against the California Angels on August 1, 1997. His dream of playing major league ball, once so unlikely, had actually come true. Scott had gone from the sandlots and poverty to the big time in Chicago.

Focus? ADD and Meds

Scott still didn't know anything about ADD. He had made it all the way to the majors on sheer will. Then one day in 2002, after five years in the big leagues, Scott casually asked one of his teammates what the pill he took every day was for. The teammate explained to him that it was for ADD. The pill helped him focus.

Scott didn't think much about that until he read a quote from himself in the newspaper. Explaining a shaky outing he had just had, Scott told a reporter, "I lost focus out there."

Abruptly, he remembered the words of his teammate. He spoke to the team doctor, who had already noticed things about Scott—hyperactivity, distractibility—that made him suspect Scott had ADD. Scott consulted another doctor, one unconnected to the team, who formally diagnosed him with ADD and started him on medication.

Just as it did for his teammate, the medication allowed Scott to focus more consistently. It surprised Scott that there was a diagnosis and a treatment to explain why schoolwork had been so hard, why he had always been a little spacey, a little antsy, and a little off balance. With medication and some behavioral tools to help him focus, Scott was delighted that he was more consistently able to "be there," not only in ball games, but also with his wife and their two kids.

Looking Back

While he was able to focus before well enough to make it all the way to the majors, Scott was doing so at great expense, putting in tremendous effort without even knowing that he was working at a disadvantage, as if he were driving a car with square wheels. In all areas of his life, he had to force himself to pay attention. He didn't realize that this was not "normal," because he had never known anything different.

Struggling in school, trying as hard as he could to stay focused but not being able to—this was "normal" as far as Scott knew. He had no idea that while others were gliding along smoothly in life, he was bumping along. He had no idea that forgetting his homework in fifth grade day after day meant anything other than not trying hard enough, as teachers had told him, or that feeling confused in math class meant anything other than his lack of math skills. Treating his ADD gave him a brand-new set of wheels, round wheels.

It would have been great if Scott could have known about his ADD back when he was in school. School would have been easier for him, and he would have liked himself better. He has done well because he has a great mother, a great dream, and great strength of character, but he also had to work doubly hard.

When People Put Me Down

In his own words, Scott says he has come so far because of "God-given talent."

"Seriously," he says. "That has a lot to do with it. But then, you know, I had a little determination, especially when someone said I couldn't do it. I had people say, 'Well, you might be a good Double A or Triple A pitcher, but probably not in the big leagues.' Then when I got to the big leagues, they said, 'Well, you might do all right, but you'll probably end up being sent down.' And then when I stayed, they had nothing to say. When people put me down, it made me work harder."

Scott speaks freely about having ADD and taking medication. "If some little kid is going to take his medicine because of me, a major league player who takes it, then I have done a good thing," Scott says. "I'm not a big-name player by any means. I'm not one of the superstars that everybody has heard of. But I am a major leaguer and kids look up to all of us, both the big stars and players like me. If I can put that respect to good use by helping a kid feel okay about having ADD, then I think that's pretty good." Scott's increased focus has led to stints on the San Francisco Giants, and most recently, to a big trade to the Chicago Cubs.

Scott's already seen how much difference he's making by being open about having ADD. "I was running down to the bull pen one day," he says, "when I looked over into the stands, and there was a kid waving at me. He was holding up a sign. As I got closer, I could read it. It said, 'I have ADD. Thank you.'"

CAROLYN O'NEAL

Retired School Principal

Think how lucky you are! ADD has done more to get me where I am than it has hindered me.

Date of Birth: March 17, 1943
Elgin, Illinois

EVERYONE IN CAROLYN O'NEAL'S FAMILY, for as far back as she can recount, has prized education. "My great-grandfather on my mother's side was brought North by a white family that educated him," Carolyn says. "I don't think he was a slave, but his parents probably were." Her great-grandmother on her father's side was a teacher. Carolyn's dad didn't finish high school—but he worked three jobs and kept a small farm to make sure all six of his children had a chance to go as far as they could. "Education was an expectation," Carolyn says. "It wasn't *if* you go to college, but *when* you go to college." All but one of her sisters and brothers earned college degrees, and one went to law school.

Like everyone else in her family, Carolyn felt passionately about education. Her college degree was in math education. She taught math for years, then went back to school so that

15

she could get certified to work as an elementary school principal, a job she held for more than ten years. What she wanted more than anything, though, was to get a doctorate, or PhD, the highest degree in a university that it is possible to earn. Carolyn enrolled to get a PhD in educational administration. A straight-A student in high school who had distinguished herself in college, Carolyn expected that if she worked hard, she'd experience success as usual. When that didn't happen, Carolyn began to unravel.

ADD in the Person in Charge

Carolyn finished the course work for her PhD during the school year and summers and then struggled to pass her qualifying exams. When she reached the stage at which she needed to write a book-length essay, or dissertation, Carolyn stalled. "I did a lot of research," Carolyn remembers, but she just could not get through the writing, which required her to sit quietly and independently, pulling together thousands of bits of information. "The paper got further and further away," she says. After six years, Carolyn couldn't justify the cost of enrolling in school. "I finally just didn't do it anymore. It was a waste of money." To those looking in from the outside, Carolyn's unfinished degree wasn't so strange, really, given that Carolyn was married, raising three kids, and working full-time. "But I really started to question my ability. I felt like I was a failure," she says. "It seemed like I couldn't deal with things anymore. I was still going to work every day. Nobody said, 'What's wrong?' or anything. Apparently, everything looked the same on the outside. But inside, it felt at any second as if a rubber band was stretched and going to pop."

You'd think that if anyone could have put the clues together, it would have been an elementary school principal. You know—the person in charge. The one who's seen it all. Who has a handle on *everything*.

But Carolyn just blamed herself. The only way she could explain what she perceived as failure, the only way she could account for her feelings, was to conclude that she just wasn't working hard enough. That's the nature of ADD, though—even for school principals. You don't know anything's wrong, because the feelings of anxiety, blame, and failure seem "normal." It never occurs to you that your brain might not be working as well in some areas as it could. It never occurs to you that you might need a little help.

Checkbook? Laundry? Help!

Despite her obvious intelligence, academic successes, and ability to connect to all kinds of people, Carolyn had always been disorganized and had acted without thinking things through. She married and had a daughter at eighteen. No doubt about it, she says, "the marriage was impulsive." Carolyn and her husband, Ron, wanted to get their college degrees, so their parents helped care for their daughter while the two kept going to school. Also an educator, Ron was her complementary opposite: organized and efficient. "He does one thing at a time," Carolyn says. "He's very structured, and he finishes everything he starts."

Not so Carolyn. Two more children later, and Carolyn's lack of organization and planning at home was making Ron nuts. It drove him crazy that their house was usually a wreck. It drove him even crazier that Carolyn could never keep the checkbook balanced—or keep track of the checks she wrote. Ron couldn't understand why Carolyn, a math major, couldn't figure out how much money they had in their checking account. It made no sense to him when they got to the end of every month and Carolyn, who was in charge of budgeting for groceries and supplies, didn't have anything more in the pantry to feed the family than pancake mix and half a box of spaghetti.

"The end of the month meant some pretty lean days," Carolyn says. "One time, we didn't have toilet paper, and we didn't have the money to buy more." She remembers crawling around in the car looking for packages of Kleenex. Laundry was even worse. "Each person in the family had seven sets of underwear," she explains. "I had to do laundry at a minimum one time a week. It would be Sunday night, and my husband would be furious because, once again, I'd forgotten the wash. No clean underwear. Then the rush would be on, so I'd do the laundry at the last minute." Carolyn proposed buying everybody extra underwear, but she knew the family didn't have the money. "Ron decided from then on that he'd do the laundry," she says. "He became the laundry person."

Their differences created plenty of strain. Carolyn felt that Ron couldn't see how hard she was trying to do what needed to be done. "He'd say I wasn't worried, that I acted like I didn't care," Carolyn remembers. But she did care. And she did worry. She just held it all inside. "That's so exhausting," she says. Their marriage survived the tension, Carolyn says, because she and Ron loved each other and were committed to their kids.

A Principal with a Messy Desk

At work, as a teacher and then as a principal, things weren't all that different from home. Carolyn's office looked as if a tornado had blown through, leaving stacked swirls of paper everywhere. She often forgot meetings. "If I came to school at seven thirty and had a meeting at ten, the meeting could come and go," Carolyn says. "If I didn't have a calendar with me when I set a date, if I didn't write it down . . ." Her voice trails off. "Well, I probably wouldn't have remembered to look at the calendar anyway." Grading, report cards, written plans—Carolyn left them all to the last minute. "If a report was due by the end of the day Friday, sometimes I'd *start* at the end of the day Friday," she says. "If I did it at the last minute, just in time to hand it in, it was always fine, or at least good enough. But I had to have the rush, the panic, to get it in," she says. "If I did things ahead of time, I'd do them to death, adding on, thinking of more things, making changes, never quite getting to the end."

Good at multitasking—*doing* more than one thing at a time—Carolyn was not so good at *finishing* more than one thing at a time. "I'd work on a lot of different things at once, but I never took one thing to completion. I'd always be going to the next thing. Everything was open. Nothing had closure. I'd have ten things ongoing without anything finished."

Strengths That Really Counted

As a school principal, Carolyn's saving grace was that she was allowed to hire a secretary. "She would think of me as loosey-goosey," Carolyn says. "And I thought of her as just rigid. But we complemented each other, were a good balance for each other." Carolyn says her secretary thought of everything in terms of "problems that needed fixing." Meanwhile, Carolyn tended to let things go, approaching them more creatively without the sense that everything was a dire emergency. "She says I changed her, made her a different person," Carolyn recalls. That's probably true in reverse, as well, Carolyn admits. Without her secretary, Carolyn says, she would have been lost.

Carolyn was so extraordinarily good with people that those around her at work tended to forgive her chaos. "I had strengths in things that really counted," Carolyn says. "I guess it was sort of written across my forehead that I could be empathetic, that people could talk to me. Children would come in and tell me something, and there was no name-calling, no put-downs. I did my job as principal very well, and I got good evaluations. I did well with staff and students and parents."

ADD: Piecing Together the Clues

Even though Carolyn felt great about herself at school, she still felt rotten that she hadn't managed to tackle the PhD. A member of the African Methodist Episcopal Church, Carolyn had gone to church her whole life. "When I grew up, nobody went to see a doctor for feelings," Carolyn says. "You'd just get your act together. People would just say, 'You don't need a psychologist or a psychiatrist, you need God.'" No matter how much Carolyn went to church, she couldn't shake feelings of depression or make herself feel better. "I didn't know what to pray for," she says, because she didn't know what it was she was asking for or what was wrong.

Carolyn finally figured things out, not at church, but at school. The administrators and teachers at her elementary school were at a workshop—something "lighthearted," Carolyn says, "to help us get through the year." Everyone was supposed to say something about themselves that no one else knew. Standing in a circle, one teacher said that he had ADD and that when he was little, he was "just like one of the kids who has you pulling your hair out all the time." The substitute teacher chimed in, saying that she had ADD, too. Afterward, Carolyn confronted this woman. "I said, 'What on earth would make you get a diagnosis of ADD? You don't seem hyperactive. Were you diagnosed as a kid?' And she said, 'No, I was diagnosed maybe two years ago.'" Carolyn asked her what her "symptoms" were. "She said she was disorganized, forgetful, that she procrastinated, that she couldn't keep her house clean, that she didn't have a sense of time. I laughed at her, joking, and said, 'Well, if *you* have ADD, then so do I.' And she said to me, seriously, 'I know, but I didn't know if I should say anything or not. I mean, the way your office is and everything.'"

Carolyn was stunned.

The substitute teacher wasn't kidding. She really thought Carolyn had ADD.

Deep Breath and a Diagnosis

Once Carolyn had caught her breath, she started asking questions. Carolyn learned that it's not just kids who have ADD—adults have it, too, and take medicine and get counseling and feel better. Carolyn took the name of the substitute teacher's doctor. After thinking it through, she gave him a call. "I told him the story," she says. "He wanted to make sure I wasn't taking on the symptoms of someone else." The doctor gave Carolyn lots of tests and even went so far as to make her husband and parents fill out questionnaires. When she came to meet with him to get the testing results, Carolyn learned that, in fact, she did have ADD. "He told me I was a *classic* example of a woman with ADD—the inattentive type. He explained to me that the kinds of problems I was experiencing tended to be what girls experienced. He said that boys with ADD tend to have shorter fuses and more outbursts, but that girls hold everything in, not letting other people know how hard it is to keep everything together."

Even though most everyone who knew her found it hard to believe she had ADD, Carolyn decided she wanted to follow the doctor's suggestions and figure out what was going on. She agreed to try Ritalin and to keep coming to counseling. She was nothing short of amazed to find that both made her feel so much better. "The diagnosis was just a tremendous relief," she remembers. "I did a lot of crying. I forgave myself and accepted myself. I had been stressed every day because my office wasn't neat. But I realized, 'It's *my* office.' I didn't let things go, I just looked at them differently. I would say to myself, 'This isn't one of my strengths, but I have other strengths.'"

Carolyn also started reading everything she could about ADD. She joined CHADD, the national nonprofit organization representing children and adults with ADD, and she went to one of its annual conferences. Sitting with all sorts of people with ADD at the conference, Carolyn says she felt absolutely wonderful: "It was the same feeling I felt when I went to Jamaica for the first time. It was the first time I'd ever been in the majority before. It was a feeling that everybody was like *me*. I just felt it in the air."

PhD: Reaching for the Stars

In counseling after the diagnosis, Carolyn realized that one of the things that still upset her was not having completed her doctorate. "I had done all that work and had spent all that money and time, and I had nothing to show for it. I always had it in the pit of my stomach." As Carolyn started to feel better, and she started to understand herself better, she decided that she wanted to try again. She found a different program and picked a new topic. She decided to write her dissertation on elementary school children who had ADD but hadn't been diagnosed. "I really felt a lot of compassion for children who had ADD. I could see they were smart kids, but they just couldn't get it together in class." Passionate about her subject, able to focus and organize better with the help of medication, Carolyn completed her degree in 2001 through Loyola University in Chicago. She recently retired from her job as principal and is now working part-time as an educational consultant, is enjoying a wide variety of volunteer positions, and loves spending time with her family.

The Blessings of ADD

Carolyn says she thinks her three grown children have learned a lot from what she's been through. They've gotten over any fears of seeking help from a counselor. "I had such good results from counseling. If there's anything, I told them, go to a psychologist." In addition, after finding out about Carolyn's diagnosis, two of her kids—Carolyn's oldest daughter and her son—saw doctors where they live and were told that they, too, have ADD. Two of Carolyn's grandsons also have been diagnosed with ADD. It clearly runs in the family, Carolyn says, and she's actually glad about it.

"I told them, 'Think how lucky you are!' ADD has done more to get me where I am than it has hindered me," she says. "I could do so many things at once, and I could go from one thing to the other. Impulsivity is a good thing sometimes!"

DAVID NEELEMAN

Founder, Chairman, and CEO,
JetBlue Airlines

Try every day to take steps
toward achieving your goals.
And most important, believe
in yourself!

Date of Birth: October 16, 1958
New Canaan, Connecticut

DAVID NEELEMAN IS A BIG-PICTURE KIND OF GUY. Founder, chairman, and chief executive officer of JetBlue Airlines, one of the fastest-growing airlines in this country, David tends to think up solutions to problems that no one else even notices. Sometimes, because he has ADD, David also tends to ignore solutions to problems he creates—things that other people see clearly.

David's the guy who invented the electronic ticket, a way to shorten lines and long waits at airports. He's also the guy who forgot to take the chicken off the backyard barbecue grill, leaving it to turn into charcoal while he drove off to the mall to buy a new digital watch. That's the way it goes with ADD, David says. Sometimes you're on fire with energy and creativity . . . and sometimes, because you lose focus and your attention travels elsewhere, it's the barbecue grill that's on fire.

David has known for only a few years that he has ADD. Before his diagnosis, he couldn't account for his wandering mind. Now he can explain how the same brain can do so much *and* miss so much. David says he wouldn't trade it for anything in the world.

The Biggest Idiot on the Planet

That doesn't mean it's always easy to be him. When he was in school, David was convinced he was stupid. He has always had trouble reading and writing, suggesting that he may have undiagnosed dyslexia. He could rarely sit still and follow through with what teachers asked him to do. "I grew up thinking I was the biggest idiot on the planet," he says. By the time he got to high school, David was able to make decent grades, but as he says, he "wasn't taking anything hard." School just wasn't something serious to David. "I was basically BS-ing my teachers, getting through," he remembers, "but I felt very inferior."

Everything changed for David when, as a Mormon, or member of the Church of the Latter-day Saints, he was sent on a mission. Mormons generally spend two years away from home, working for their church. David went back to Brazil, where he'd been born, and learned Portuguese. "It gave me a lot of structure," he says, and that's something people with ADD need. "I was in Brazil, and I learned a foreign language." A natural salesman, David was especially good at getting people to consider becoming Mormon. "Soon I was converting people to my faith. This gave me the confidence I'd never had."

When David came home from Brazil, he once again wrestled with disorganization and restlessness. Even though he felt, inside, that he was "a changed person," he had to force himself to get through his studies at the University of Utah. "I was a tremendous procrastinator. I hated to study. I felt like I should be out doing things, moving things along, but here I was stuck studying statistics, which I knew had no application to my life," David says. "Finals would come, and I'd be up all night and cramming for this stupid stuff. I liked very little of what I was studying, but I knew I had to have an education." At the first possible opportunity, David dropped out of college and started a business. "I just blew out of there," he says, and it felt wonderful.

Brilliant Business Beginnings

The opportunity sort of fell into his lap, he says. A friend's mother knew a man who was having trouble keeping condominiums rented in Hawaii. David approached him with a business idea. He knew the man was paying $150 a month in maintenance fees for every vacant condo. He figured in exchange for finding condo renters, the man could pay *him* the $150. Married and with a child on the way, David was eager to find a way to make some money. "It was such a bizarre thing," David says. "I was renting one or two condos a day, so I was making two, three, four hundred bucks a day. I thought, 'Wow, this is good.'" In one of those big-picture moments, David thought, "Well, let me just combine the rentals with some airfare deals." He knew that there were some new airlines starting up on the West Coast, so he called and arranged to buy discounted airline tickets. Soon, he was able to package the Hawaii condo rentals with airplane tickets.

Typical of people with ADD, David struggled with academic work, but he thrived once he was out of school. That's when he could draw on the big-picture part of his brain. He has, he says, a "natural ability to know what's important," a talent for cutting "right through all the rubbish and getting to that nugget." Using his persistence and inventiveness, David is able to identify the really important things, focus on them, and decide that the "other stuff is just noise." Like many people with ADD, he thinks this is his "greatest talent."

Taking Off with Airlines

By the second year that David was packaging Hawaiian travel and condo rentals, he had hired twenty employees. "I got other condos, and it was booming," David says, but then, in a single instant, the business fell apart. "The airline called me up one day right before Christmas and said, 'We're gone.' And I said, 'What do you mean, *You're gone?*' The airline went out of business. It took all of my money. I was twenty-two years old, and I was devastated."

On the lookout for another opportunity, David leaped at

the chance to start something new. His uncle, an attorney, had a client with a successful travel business. The client proposed that David come to work for her and start an airline. "We became Morris Air," David says, "and nine years later, we sold the company to Southwest Airlines for $130 million."

From there, he went to work for Southwest Airlines, where he developed the electronic ticket. When David arrived at Southwest, passengers had to go through a complicated ticketing procedure. David suggested the company sidestep this process, allowing passengers to use their credit cards to register to fly. "It saved us tens of millions of dollars," he says.

Crash

David's quirky personality and inventiveness won him friends. His impatience and inability to deal with what he saw as obvious, picky little stuff also earned him enemies. While some at Southwest Airlines wanted to promote David to help run the company, others pushed to have him fired. The head of the company told David that he "had all these guys coming in and complaining" about him, even David's "best buddy."

David remembers this as one of the worst times of his life. "He fired me," David says. During these terrible times David read a book about ADD. He thought, "This is *me*!" David got in touch with a psychiatrist, made an appointment, and was diagnosed as having ADD.

With the diagnosis of ADD and some counseling, David began to understand why he'd had such a hard time at Southwest Airlines and why he'd been fired. He realized that his impulsivity caused him to sit in meetings and blurt out whatever came into his mind. "All these guys would be sitting at a table," David remembers, "and I would say something like, 'Geez, I just can't stand sitting here talking about pregnant ramp agents hour after hour! We should get to something important! Why are we dealing with this? Have someone else deal with that!'" Focused on the things that he thought were important, David had absolutely no patience for things he considered small potatoes. He says he would try to stop himself, but he just didn't know what to do with his powerful feelings of boredom and restlessness. David decided he did not want to take medication, fearing that it might hamper his creativity and his ability to see the big picture.

That doesn't mean David's against medication for ADD. In fact, several of his nine kids, who inherited his ADD, take medications. He has desperately wanted his children to have a better time in school than he had. He'd do anything, he says, to prevent them from feeling dumb, the way he did, but it's not easy. "Of my nine kids, nine of them struggle in school," he says. "They are really smart kids, really creative, but they just struggle." His main advice to his own kids and to all kids with ADD is to tell them to dream big dreams. "Try every day to take steps toward achieving your goals," he says, "and most important, *believe in yourself!*"

Soar!

By the time David was ready to open JetBlue, he had a much better sense of how to take advantage of the best parts of his

ADD brain—the hyperfocus and creativity—and also what he needed to do to work on—the harder, little-picture stuff. He can come up with what other people think are wacky, impractical ideas and have a better sense of how to get them on board without leaving so many hard feelings. David says he leads JetBlue in a way that lets his employees and customers know that he's paying attention to things large and small. He goes out onto the tarmac where the airplanes are, handles baggage, works behind ticket counters, and generally does whatever else he can to show that he cares about all parts of the business.

That doesn't mean he doesn't still struggle with the problems that ADD stirs up. He still has trouble showing up for meetings on time because of standard ADD pitfalls: losing his appointment book, getting absorbed in phone conversations, forgetting where he is supposed to go, misplacing his cell phone in the car. These kinds of things don't happen too often anymore, though, because he's learned to surround himself with people who, he says, help him "pick up the slack." It's all small-picture stuff to him—but it's stuff he knows he has to pay attention to because it can drive other people nuts.

The Tree: ADD at Home

It's not just people at work who have complained about David's inability to manage the small stuff. At home, David is not a tidy guy. He leaves his belongings all over the place. "My car's a wreck," he admits. "I have two weeks worth of clothes piled up by my chair right by my bed. My socks are right by my bed in the same place I leave them." But with the diagnosis of ADD, David's marriage has gotten better. His wife accepts that his mind is just going to wander, and he's going to have a hard time doing things that other people do without having to think. Of course, David's wife is more likely to be accepting of his differences when he goes out of his way to be helpful around the house.

In the small-stuff category, David tried to deal with a tree that was leaning against the side of his house for two years. He knew it was dangerous, and he knew he needed to call the tree service and have it taken down. He looked at that tree every morning from his bathroom window while he shaved, and every morning, he set his mind to call the tree service. Each night when he brushed his teeth, he saw the tree still there, and he realized another day had passed, he hadn't called the tree service, and the small stuff was just slipping through his fingers. Others offered to call the tree service for him, but David said he needed to do it himself. Finally, David came up with one of his brilliant, creative solutions. Instead of having the tree cut down, he says, "we sold the house."

Karl V. Euler V

Police Officer

I was a bright person who had to learn differently than other people.

Date of Birth: January 12, 1971
Erie, Colorado

NOBODY CALLS KARL EULER "KARL." Ever since he was a kid, his name's been "Kipp." Until recently, that is. At work at the Boulder, Colorado, police department, he's earned the nickname "Batman." Actually, it wasn't his fellow police officers who gave him the name. It was a bunch of drug dealers who liked to hang out on a hill outside of town. "I would show up, in plainclothes or in uniform, and they and their friends would disappear, just like that!" Kipp snaps his fingers and laughs. "I'd have taken them into jail in no time." After several arrests, one of the drug dealers jokingly compared Kipp to Batman. "And I said, 'No, I *am* Batman!'" Now when he needs to detain a suspect, Kipp whips out his handy Batman key chain to reach for his handcuff key.

Kipp's similarities to Bruce Wayne don't go very far— Kipp lives about fifteen miles from Denver in a house with his wife, Megan, and their newborn daughter. No cave. No butler. No Batmobile, either. Like Batman, though, Kipp's favorite part of his job requires rescue. A field training officer and crime scene investigator with the rank of detective, Kipp is also a licensed emergency medical technician, or EMT, who heads the Boulder Police Department's SWAT team. During his time off, he helps out with local emergency management, cleaning up after plane crashes, for instance. Kipp knows it's a little weird, but he loves to pull people out of rushing white water or to cut them out of mangled automobiles. "It's very fulfilling," he says. "Even saving one life is worth it."

His Parents:
The Real Superheroes

Kipp says he isn't a superhero. He's just highly trained, with good instincts, natural negotiating skills, and a great sense of humor. The real superheroes in his life, he says, are his

parents, Kathleen and Karl, rescuers in their own way. A sixth-grade teacher and a hardware store owner, respectively, they adopted Kipp as a baby. Despite his huge struggles with ADD and dyslexia, they never gave up on him. "I couldn't have asked for better parents," Kipp says. "They never faulted me for having so many difficulties. They've always told me they're extremely proud of me the way I am, even when I haven't done well. That means more to me than anything else."

Kipp describes himself as "a rubber band with hair" and "a raw, exposed nerve ending" when he was a boy growing up in Illinois. Parenting him, he says, was incredibly difficult. He was constantly moving around and fidgeting. As a baby, he wouldn't stay in his crib. "They'd find me sleeping in a chest of drawers or the sandbox," he says. "I was a wanderer." The only time he was still, he says, was when he went fishing with his dad. "I could go days and not move or get bored," he says. "There was this calming effect of being in a boat, near water, away from other people."

School was a different story altogether, Kipp says. Without assignment and organizational sheets, school "would have been a *horrible* disaster," he says, but with them, "instead, it was just a disaster." Kipp rarely did homework, constantly forgetting his books and papers at school. He collected junk, surrounding himself with what he describes as "a force field of clutter." His parents asked teachers to be understanding. "I had *two* flip-top desks at school. They gave me an extra desk to put my junk."

Not Batman Overnight: An Early Diagnosis

It's hard to imagine a police detective with such a disorganized, restless beginning. Kipp says he didn't become "Batman" overnight. It took years of effort and some exceptional guidance along the way.

Diagnosed with dyslexia and ADD in second grade, Kipp tried a wide range of approaches to improve his concentration and organization. Neither Ritalin nor diet changes were helpful. The only thing that helped was sports, especially swimming, which seemed to help Kipp handle his behavior a bit better. In junior high, Kipp tried another medication, Norpramin, an antidepressant used sometimes in the treatment of ADD. "This worked pretty well," he says. Kipp took the medicine daily through much of high school but stopped taking it, not because he outgrew ADD, but because he learned how to cope. "I don't think ADD ever goes away," he says, "but I think you figure out how to work with it, even to make it work to your advantage."

No matter what his parents tried, they could not find a way to make public school work for Kipp. By high school, Kipp would get pulled out of class into the "cross-categorical resource room," which other kids unkindly called "the retard room." This room was a place where teachers, as Kipp says, "warehoused anybody who was different." Whether kids had health issues, physical disabilities, mental health issues, autism, or dyslexia, these students were lumped together without any sense that they all needed different kinds of special education.

Boarding School

What Kipp needed, he says, was more educational support. His parents, he says, had given him everything they could. They consulted with an educational specialist, who recommended they send Kipp to the Landmark School, a boarding school in Massachusetts for kids with language-based learning disabilities. Kipp's parents were nervous about sending their son so far away, but they had run out of options. For his part, Kipp had given up. He was convinced that no matter what he did, he would fail. Kipp's parents sent him to Landmark the summer before his senior year of high school. "It was probably the most loving thing they could have done," he says.

His time at boarding school was "a tremendous growing experience," Kipp says. Courses at the school taught Kipp *how* to learn. "I felt like I had this tremendous building that had been built over no foundation," he says, "so I had missed all the basic things that I needed: organization, how to study, how to actually take the work from point A to the finish." With the right kind of help, Kipp says, he was able to begin to learn on his own and succeed. The teachers were relaxed and knew how to have fun. "They were just goofy," Kipp says. "They obviously had a great time teaching. I mean, they took their teaching very seriously, but you'd never have known it. They made it all look like easy fun." Kipp says being around these kinds of teachers was "a huge revelation. They were more like friends than teachers. I could turn to them for help and advice. I looked up to them. What good people!"

At College:
Still Not Quite Batman

When it was time for Kipp to graduate, he was actually ready for college. With help from guidance counselors at Landmark, he picked a small college in New Hampshire with a good resource center for students with learning disabilities. "The first semester, I spent a lot of time at the study skills center," Kipp remembers. "Basically, I used it to get used to college life. I didn't know quite how to handle college courses. There was so much freedom. There was no one asking to see homework, and if it didn't work out . . . oh, well." It took him a few semesters, but soon he was relying less on the resource center and tutorials and more on himself, and with the exception of a few Cs, he usually made more As than Bs. "With study skills I became an excellent student," Kipp says. "It reinforced what my parents had been telling me all those years. I was a bright person who had to learn differently than other people."

Inspired by his time at boarding school, Kipp decided to major in education and, with newfound confidence, reached out at college, taking leadership positions on campus, joining a coed fraternity, and working part-time, trying to earn a little money. The job he took was filling in part-time as a security guard.

Life with Batgirl

Best, he says, is that he found a new girlfriend. He walked into a restaurant his freshman year and was instantly smitten by the young woman at the counter. "I went in and asked for a hamburger, fries, and her phone number," Kipp says. "She sent me packing. After being crushed and humiliated publicly, I left." He ran into her crossing a covered bridge on foot later in the semester. Dying to escape but with nowhere to hide, he stuck out his hand. It turned out that she was a member of the fraternity he'd pledged, and she'd already requested to serve as his "big sister." She hadn't remembered the incident at the restaurant but had seen him around and wanted to get to know him. "That's how I met Megan. We dated all through college. I knew, and so did she, within the first week of dating that we were going to end up married. We were just right. She has tons and tons of energy, and she's always been so supportive of me."

After college, Kipp and Megan married and looked for work in New Hampshire. Kipp tried teaching but could find work only part-time as a substitute. Not knowing day to day what his schedule would be, Kipp felt anxious and restless all the time. Still working as a security officer to make money, he noted that a friend who was working as an EMT seemed to be enjoying himself and getting paid well. This friend convinced Kipp to give it a try. Kipp surprised himself by doing extremely well on the tests he had to take to become an EMT. Once he was certified, Kipp provided life support and prehospital care for people who'd been shot by a gun, had had heart attacks or strokes, had been bitten by dogs, had been in bad car wrecks, or had suffered any accident or illness that required hospitalization.

A Police Officer with a Sense of Humor

When Kipp and Megan moved to Colorado so that Megan could take a job as a professional stage manager, Kipp wasn't sure, at first, what kind of work he wanted to find. To help pay the rent, he took a job doing something familiar—patrolling a mall in Boulder as a security officer. There, he worked alongside police officers, helping them arrest shoplifters, deal with fights, and settle gang disputes.

One day, a police officer pulled him aside. "He said, 'What are you doing here? You're wasting your time doing security work. Why don't you think about becoming a police officer?'" Kipp decided to give it a try. He started in a group of about sixty recruits. Thanks to his hard work at boarding school and in college, he easily passed exams in math, reading, and writing. He had to take psychological tests and type a certain number of words a minute. These, too, weren't hard for Kipp. Not surprisingly, Kipp breezed through the physical fitness tests. At each step along the way, the police department weeded out people who couldn't perform well. Kipp made each and every cut. When he found out he'd been selected to become a police officer, Kipp was stunned. "I was so excited, I couldn't believe it!" he says. "I had passed all that testing and gotten hired. It blew my mind."

Soon Kipp was out in the community, and he found that he absolutely loved the work. "You're going up to people you don't know and challenging them on what they're doing wrong," Kipp says. "You're dealing with some of these folks in the worst moments of their lives." Kipp says it's a tremendous challenge to deal well with all these crises, but with humor, he calms down everybody and convinces them not to get violent.

A Police Officer with ADD

In a funny way, Kipp says, ADD actually helps him be a good police officer and rescuer. "I'll be driving down the street, and you know, I've got the attention span of a gnat," he says. "Something will catch my attention—something most people wouldn't observe or hear. I'm constantly scanning. I think that's a gift." Kipp says he can watch the street even when he's in his cruiser carrying on a conversation with a fellow officer and listening to the radio, the police radio, and the fire channel.

Though in school settings Kipp found himself impulsive and distractible, in emergency situations he is laser sharp and focused. "It's not what you'd expect," he says. "I don't like flying, I'm not a bungee jumper, and I'm not a big risk taker. I'm not unnecessarily reckless." The excitement of dangerous, life-and-death decision making keeps Kipp's mind on target. His physical and mental speed allow him to make critical decisions quickly—but not so quickly that he's jeopardizing people's lives. It's possible, he says, that because of ADD, he can size up the risk potential more quickly than others can.

Ongoing Challenges

Staying organized continues to be tough for Kipp, but at work, he says, he seems to be able to keep track of important information. "I have to force myself," he says. "There's just no room for disorganization in police work as far as I'm concerned." It's not just written reports and incidents Kipp has to keep track of. If he's investigating a crime scene, for instance, he might have to examine a one-foot section of carpeting, getting on his hands and knees with tweezers, Kipp says, "looking with a magnifying glass for hair fibers, tiny little bits of evidence (such as blood), or hairs the bad guy left behind." It's Kipp's job to make sure everything is labeled and accounted for. Not a problem for Batman, of course, but not an easy task for a person who, once upon a time, needed two flip-top desks to hold all of his stuff. His hard work has not gone unnoticed. Recently, Kipp was promoted to Detective and became the Assistant Chief of Boulder Emergency Squad.

He still has an excess of stuff, Kipp says. He just keeps it at home with Megan. He's got bins of flashlights, sirens, pens, watches, bolts, washers, pocketknives, off-duty gun holsters—gadgets of every kind. Sure, Kipp says, he *could* throw it all out, but he doesn't want to, because "it could be handy someday." Kipp manages to separate work and home, staying hyperfocused at the police department, allowing himself to revert to his natural tendencies when off duty.

When he was a kid, Kipp wouldn't have imagined he could do both of these things—stay organized at work and be kind of messy at home. That's the trick, though, Kipp says. Don't think that just because you've got ADD, you can't figure out how to "work with it, even to make it work to your advantage." And for heaven's sake, he says, don't let ADD prevent you from trying what interests you. "I think *any* career can be good for people with ADD," Kipp says, so long as they know how to deal well. "I don't think any kids should ever limit themselves on what job to take because of ADD."

HEATHER LONG

Graduate Student, Rhodes Scholar

I see people who are brilliant and don't try. I think, "If you would just harness it, you'd ignite a fire, you'd have a big explosion."

Date of Birth: March 20, 1982
Oxford, England

TAKING A BREAK AT HOME in Mechanicsburg, Pennsylvania, from her studies at Oxford University in England, Heather Long is reading a finance textbook. Heather has just finished the first of two years as a Rhodes Scholar, one of thirty-two students chosen from an exceptional group of about one thousand college seniors to study for free at one of the world's finest universities. Wouldn't she rather be watching TV or hanging out at the pool on this gorgeous summer day? Absolutely not, Heather says. She's doing what she's wanted to do her whole life. For as long as she can remember, Heather has loved to think. Ideas are what excite her. Heather has also spent the better part of her young life figuring out how to communicate her great ideas when neither school systems nor her brain were eager to pitch in.

ADD, Dyslexic, and Brilliant

When Heather still had not begun reading in the second grade, her parents were sure there was a reason—and they knew it wasn't because Heather wasn't smart. With an offbeat sense of humor and an endless imagination, she could talk circles around other kids her age. After questioning Heather's second-grade teacher, Heather's parents took her for special tests to figure out what was going on. Yes, the tests indicated, Heather was brilliant. They also showed that she had dyslexia (a learning disorder that made it hard for her to read and write), had trouble with "working memory" (the ability to keep things front and center in her mind), and had ADD. "None of these things alone was such a big deal," Heather says. "But all three together were trouble."

The diagnosis of ADD made sense to Heather's parents. Left-handed, red haired, blue eyed, and passionate, Heather had always been an active mischief maker and risk taker. At three, she had broken her collarbone while riding her tricycle. She played so hard that her knees were always skinned, and her pants always had holes in them. "I was really into the sandbox," Heather says, chortling. "I just wasn't into keeping the *sand* in the sandbox!"

The Dreaded Tutor

Heather's parents decided they could help Heather with her ADD on their own, keeping her involved in dance and sports, but they wanted Heather to have special help for her other learning differences. Above grade level in math but behind in reading, writing, and spelling, Heather was frustrated in school. Her parents hired a tutor to work with her, and her mom helped with homework every day after school.

Heather met with the tutor about twice a week during the school year, three times a week in summer. Although Heather hated getting tutored, she knew it made a big difference. "It was a gradual process. There was a lot of rote memorization and repetition," Heather recalls. Bit by bit, she got better at recalling facts, reading, and writing.

ADD:
Phaseouts Within Phaseouts

On some level, Heather understood even as a kid that her ADD didn't just have to do with her need to move and be active. By fourth or fifth grade, she says, she had a sense that she could get distracted really easily. Heather says having ADD is like having a car radio constantly changing stations in her head: "It's like not being able to settle on one song all the way through." She also talks about ADD in terms of "phaseouts." Everybody, she says, has moments when their minds drift. "But me, I phase out within my phaseouts." Although she started out doing homework with her mom at the kitchen table, she came to see that this was just too hard for her.

Heather did everything she could to make a space for herself where it was least likely that her brain would go a-wandering. That meant no television, telephone, or radio in her bedroom.

Even though Heather worked hard to figure out how to learn, there were times when she felt embarrassed. When the kids in her class at school were flipping pages in books during silent reading, but Heather, slowed by ADD and dyslexia, was still stumbling through the first paragraph on the first page, she sometimes felt dumb. By fourth grade, when teachers expected students to hand in reports on the books they'd read, Heather wrote about *The Wizard of Oz* and *Alice in Wonderland*. "Not that I'd *read* them," Heather says, rolling her eyes. She'd *acted* in them. "I'd be dancing around questions," she says, "because there were differences between the books and the plays."

Gifted and Talented

Things got better in middle school, Heather says, because her teachers recommended her for a small gifted and talented program, capping classes at ten to twelve students. "The teachers were fantastic," she says. "They were interested in different ways of learning. There was a lot more creativity involved, so it was much easier for me to excel." Heather came into her own when teachers gave her options other than writing essays to complete assignments. When she was able to make dramatic presentations or hand in art projects that allowed her to think and produce creatively, Heather could get out her interesting thoughts without wrestling with written language or rigid structures. As a result, she was able to make straight As.

Although Heather had a great time learning and think-ing in the gifted and talented group, she had a hard time making friends. A self-described "teacher's pet," Heather says it was hard to connect with other kids her age—especially girls. She had one best friend in middle school. They both liked sappy oldies music and imaginary games. She remembers what she calls "birthday party season," when she wasn't invited to a single party. "I was marked as differ-ent. I was less interested in what other girls were interested in—things like boys and gossip. I wasn't into training bras," she cracks up, "or who had their period, or who was going out with whom."

Heather says she always found it easier to relate to adults than kids. Fascinated by what was going on in the world, Heather loved getting to talk and listen at her parents' fre-quent dinner parties. There, she says, guests discussed poli-tics, art, travel, and business, all things that captured her attention and imagination. "By fifth or sixth grade, I wanted to be a nun so I could be a missionary in Latin America. Then I wanted to live in Alaska. Every two months I had a new interest—American Indian novels, slave women—I was all over the place." What stayed constant was Heather's passion for new ideas.

No More Gifted and Talented

When Heather was about to start high school, her parents an-nounced that they were moving the family to central Penn-sylvania so that her dad could take a new job. Heather was mostly relieved, hoping she could enjoy a fresh start and make new friends. But that didn't happen. Heather kept busy, all the same, playing field hockey, playing violin in the school orchestra, and singing and acting in school musicals. Having heard Venezuelan girls speaking Spanish at a summer horseback riding camp, Heather decided she wanted to learn Spanish—not an easy task for a dyslexic. She also took Advanced Placement, or AP, classes, which allowed her to do college-level work.

Bigger than the loss Heather felt socially was the loss she experienced leaving behind the middle school gifted and talented program. She needed to be in a small group where other kids cared passionately about thinking and questioning. To be admitted to the high school's gifted and talented program in the tenth grade, Heather had to take an IQ test, a way of measuring certain kinds of intelligence, and score at least 130. "I didn't make it to one hundred and thirty," Heather says. Not knowing Heather had ADD and was dyslexic, the teacher was stunned. She had been teaching Heather for a year and could see for herself that Heather could work and think brilliantly. The few kids Heather liked and had started to get to know made it into the program.

Heather's mom decided it was time to go tell the teachers about Heather's learning differences. She wanted them to understand why Heather's scores had been lower than they'd expected. The teachers listened and offered Heather a spot in the enrichment program, but by then, Heather didn't want to participate. "I just didn't feel worthy," she says. "It was such a blow to my self-confidence."

College: A Whole New World

When it came time to apply for college, Heather wasn't sure where she wanted to go or what she wanted to study. Once again, she was faced with having to take a standardized test (this time the Scholastic Aptitude Test, or SAT), and her scores weren't terrific. She learned about Wellesley, a superb women's college located outside of Boston. Heather loved the idea of being in a place where the classes were small and the professors were devoted to helping young women succeed. She was thrilled when Wellesley accepted her.

Heather started at Wellesley thinking she would major in economics. She'd always been great with numbers, and she thought economics would help her understand how the world works. At the same time, she continued taking English classes, loving to read and think about literature even though, because of dyslexia, it took her so much extra work and patience to succeed. "I was afraid I couldn't compete," she says. It was scary to struggle with works in Old English while her classmates would whiz through the course work. She had survived a first-year writing class but had had knots in her stomach the whole time. "We had to read out loud together," Heather remembers. "I changed words around. I had to reread sentences I had already read. I felt like I was already failing." True to form, Heather stuck with it. "I didn't declare myself as an English major until the last minute," Heather says.

Course work wasn't the only great thing about college. Heather finally found the friends she'd dreamed about. Heather's friends were musicians, mathematicians, artists— they all shared a passion for ideas. In college, Heather no longer had to feel awkward about loving to think and wanting to achieve. She played violin and harpsichord, won a spot on the varsity fencing team, joined student government, and at times held down a job thirty hours a week. Heather spent her last year of college in Pamplona, Spain, where she practiced speaking Spanish and studied Spanish literature.

Behind the Wall

One of Heather's favorite activities during college was a volunteer job she took at a women's prison. She had heard that the inmates wanted to publish their own newspaper, *Behind the Wall*, so she agreed to serve as editor. Heather had gone into the prison seeing only differences. She was a college student with endless possibilities stretching out in front of her. The inmates were stuck in jail, wondering if they'd ever have a chance to do anything interesting. Heather quickly realized that she and many of the women had something in common: learning differences. While Heather had rarely shared information about having dyslexia and ADD at Wellesley, she opened up with the inmates. "It was great for me," she remembers. "We'd talk, and I'd give them creative writing assignments. I told them, 'Hey, if you can talk about it, you can write about it!' You know, it was all about self-confidence."

Losing Composure and Winning a Rhodes Scholarship

As her time at Wellesley was coming to a close, Heather thought about scholarships to do graduate work, especially ones that would allow her to study English literature *in* England. Although Heather knew how hard it would be to win one of these scholarships, she decided to give it a try. "I figured my chances were slightly better than winning at Tri-State Power Ball," she says, giving a loopy grin. She spoke with her parents, and they urged her to take that chance. She asked them if they thought she should include information about dyslexia and ADD. They warned her away from this, telling her that the selection committee might exclude her just because of her learning differences, which it might think of as unconquerable learning *disabilities*. Heather's parents feared that the committee would think that a learning disabled, or LD, student couldn't possible handle the work at a place like Oxford.

Even though Heather had decided not to share information about her learning differences with selection committees, she found herself talking about ADD and dyslexia in her interview for a Rhodes Scholarship. "There I was, in this not-warm-and-fuzzy place, and the interviewers were asking me why I had taken so many economics classes and then shifted to English," Heather remembers.

To Heather's surprise, she lost her composure. "I got really choked up," she says. Everything came pouring out—her struggles learning to read and write, her loss of self-confidence, and her fears about deciding to study English. She was able to pull it all together by explaining why she wanted to connect her fascination with money and economic markets to novels and publishing, all of which she hoped would help her work as a journalist for a financial newspaper. As she left the interview, Heather wondered if she'd blown it.

On the contrary, she continued to advance in the competition until she learned about midway through her senior year that, indeed, she had been selected to study at Oxford as a Rhodes Scholar. "It was a really neat feeling," Heather says. "It was great to realize all the ways I had been coping, how many ways I had adjusted. Maybe to compensate for having ADD I've overfocused. You know, even when classes were boring, and other people were nodding off, I was still right there. Because it's all or nothing for me. If I miss the moment, it's gone. It's not going to come back."

Coming to Terms with LD

After she found out about winning the Rhodes, Heather went home to celebrate with her family. Her mom pulled out old test reports and school records. They talked about what it meant to be super smart *and* to have learning differences. "I can weave this ribbon through my life. I have an explanation," she says, "that helps me understand why I am the way I am."

Heather's advice to kids with ADD is to accept that they aren't necessarily limited. "It's not the end," she says. "You have to be creative and find ways to utilize your strengths within the system. You can't give up."

Don't take standardized tests too seriously, she also advises. "So, you didn't get a thousand six hundred on your SATs," she says, referring to a perfect score. "So what? You can still be an accomplished person." Those test scores don't reveal much about potential, she says. "I see people who are brilliant and don't try. I think, 'If you would just harness it, you'd ignite a fire, you'd have a big explosion.'"

In her case, she says, she's always had to work harder than everyone else, but maybe that's not such a bad thing. Having ADD and being dyslexic have "helped me," Heather says. "They have made me more disciplined. It's been hard since the beginning. But I see how far I *have* come."

Devin M. Barclay

Professional Soccer Player,
Columbus Crew

Recess was it *for me. I'd get
to* run. *Running around
and playing on the blacktop,
I'd get to totally unleash.*

Date of Birth: April 9, 1983
Columbus, Ohio

DEVIN BARCLAY HAS TWO STORIES TO TELL. Neither makes
sense without the other. A professional soccer player, Devin
speaks openly about the pure joy of running after a ball. A
young adult with ADD, he also talks about the delights and
difficulties of being different.

Devin has been kicking a ball from the time he could
walk. "When I really started playing, I was about four," he
says. His dad, David, set up a small goal in their basement. If
Devin hit the center of the net, the goal would make a loud
noise. "I started kicking the ball too hard for that and breaking windows and stuff down there, so we moved it to the
street. As soon as we moved it, my dad would roll me the ball,
and I would kick it, and that was just the *best* thing for me.
I *loved* to kick the ball . . . kicking the ball as hard as I could.
That was the awesomest thing." That love carried Devin from

organized youth leagues to competitive regional teams to the Olympic Development Program, all the way to Major League Soccer (MLS). A professional player, first in Tampa Bay, Florida, then in San Jose, California, next in Washington, DC, Devin currently lives in Columbus, Ohio, where he plays for the Crew. Devin has played matches in Portugal, Germany, France, Italy, England, Chile, Mexico, Canada, Holland, Spain, and the United Arab Emirates.

The Agony of Defeat

Not everything has been as much fun for Devin as playing soccer. From as early as kindergarten, Devin had a hard time learning. "I was *always* having trouble paying attention," he says. "I can remember my kindergarten year, and I can remember having to do math problems and not being able to finish them. When you finished, you could go out for recess, so I remember not being able to finish. You know, I couldn't do the problem right. And recess was *it* for me. I'd get to *run*. Running around and playing on the blacktop, I'd get to totally unleash." Not being able to finish his math, Devin wasn't able to get outside to play. That was a particularly painful early lesson to learn about school. "The reason why I'm so enthusiastic about soccer is that it was the only thing that came easy for me."

By second grade, Devin was miserable in school. His parents had him tested for learning differences. "I saw three different doctors who all said the same thing, which was that I was very ADD," Devin remembers. "They said they wanted to put me on medication right away." Devin started taking Ritalin. He says he never thought of Ritalin as medicine because his doctors called it "the thinking pill."

Homework Headaches

Even with Ritalin, Devin continued to have a hard time in school. He hated doing homework, and he needed lots of help from his parents to finish his assignments. His younger brother, Colin, who does not have ADD, would quickly finish his homework on his own, while Devin spent hours with his parents trying to understand his reading and do his math. "I never ever ever did my homework correctly," he recalls. "I always did it wrong. That was hard for me. I always wanted to be done with it and *run*. The reality of it was that I wouldn't be done until bedtime because it would take so long. I would literally have fits—temper tantrums—because I could never do it correctly."

Devin says that through eighth grade, he was willing to try because his parents and teachers made him feel that

they wanted him to do well. "I don't remember ever thinking that I was stupid. My parents were so supportive. They would never say anything to make me feel stupid. I had a lot of security from home, which always helps." In addition, he knew his teachers were cheering him on: "They understood that I had a problem, and they gave me the help that I needed." That kept Devin from hating school. He had good friends and spent his free time at lunch, recess, and after school playing soccer.

Hating High School

Things were different when Devin headed to high school. A private school recruited Devin to play soccer, but it insisted he repeat the eighth grade. The work was harder, teachers were less flexible, and Devin lost patience. "That was where things really started to go downhill," he says. Devin couldn't keep up with the work. He had a lot of trouble remembering what he was asked to read. He couldn't pay attention in class or take notes, which made homework even harder. He knew he was capable of focusing on and remembering what he read, but that only seemed to happen when he found the subjects interesting enough to hold his attention.

"The funny thing is—when I learned about something that interested me, I did really well, and I could concentrate. When it sunk in, I was just as smart as anyone else. Even now, if you give me a book to read about surfing or soccer or something that interests me, I'll be able to explain in general what it was about," he says. "But I was reading about things I didn't care about. So I didn't remember any of it. Good Lord, if someone asked me a question about it, I wouldn't know anything, because I'd be thinking about going outside and biking or playing soccer. It was just so bad because I couldn't do what they wanted me to do."

Finding His Inner Beckham

Two things happened to turn things around for Devin. First, he hit puberty. He got bigger and stronger and faster. He started lifting weights. Second, he decided to stop taking Ritalin. Devin believes that rather than helping him concentrate and think, Ritalin made him feel depressed and droopy. Unfortunately, his behavior at school wasn't so good without the medicine. He acted up in class and also cheated on tests. He's not proud of these things, but he realized that without the medicine, he was a livelier, more energetic soccer player. "That's when I really started to turn the corner," he says. "That's when I really started to dominate in sports—when I came off of Ritalin. That's when I made the national team."

Devin says that his parents were upset that he was so unhappy at school. His father is a lawyer, and his mother helps run a middle school. His brother is a gifted student. It was hard for them to accept that for Devin, formal education in a school setting wasn't working out. "They knew it wasn't for me. They knew it was painful for me, and they knew I did not want to be doing what I was doing," he says. They encouraged him to try using special tutors and talking to a counselor. Devin did both, but even then, he says, "None of it really worked for me."

Leaving High School, Playing Soccer

When Devin was in the tenth grade, U.S. coaches asked him to play soccer on the national team. That's when he realized he had a chance to play professional soccer. He even tried playing for a British "football club" (competitive soccer team). In December 2000, when he was sixteen, Devin signed a special contract for young players with Major League Soccer that promised him six years of training and competition. "It was the easiest decision in the world for me. Because when somebody says at the end of the day, 'You can go and play soccer for two hours and then for the rest of the day you'll get paid for that,' that was like God saying, 'Son, I bless you!' It was *great*. It was the *best thing* in the world. I was *so* excited. It was my dream come true." Devin left school and earned a high school diploma by getting tutored.

These days, Devin gets up early to be with his dogs, Lola, a five-month-old Yorkie-Pomeranian mix, and Becks, a one-and-a-half-year old German shepherd–Rottweiler mix. He spends about half an hour eating breakfast and getting showered, watches sports on television, and then heads for practice. During the week he works with his teammates from about 11:00 a.m. to 1:30 p.m. After practice, his day is his own. He's not so relaxed on the weekends, when he plays soccer matches. Then the pressure to win can get him pretty anxious.

Devin has been working in Columbus with his team's chaplain as a part of Athletes in Action, a group offering Christian teachings to kids who play sports. Devin helps run soccer camps at churches, where he has a chance to help kids develop soccer skills and talk about the Bible and the importance of Jesus and faith in his own life.

College Bound?

Nearing the end of his sixth year as an MLS player, Devin doesn't know whether he'll continue to have a contract in 2006 to play soccer professionally. He's had to fight for playing time during games and has most recently been playing weekly matches on the Crew's reserve team, the soccer equivalent to AAA minor league teams in baseball. "I feel really good physically. I'm taking care of my body, and I'm just happy to be out there, staying healthy, doing what I love." If MLS management and the Crew don't renew his contract, Devin is thinking about doing something really radical—at least, radical for him.

Devin is coming to realize that "success" may have more to do with flexibility than just playing soccer. Devin is thinking about going to college. "My first choice would be to continue to play soccer because I've invested so much of my time in it. I still *love* the sport," he says, "but given the opportunity to do something else, I think I'd like to go to college."

Friends Devin has made through his Bible-study group and his work with Athletes in Action have encouraged Devin to reconsider his options. "They've helped me see that there are other things out there besides soccer that I could be doing and be happy." His mom and dad have also continued to be supportive, giving Devin room to think about what he wants to do with his life.

Athletics rules allow Devin to continue to play sports in college—but not soccer. "I've been kicking field goals in my spare time," Devin says, laughing. "I still have eligibility to play other sports in college." Maybe, he says, there will be a way for him to get a scholarship to be a kicker on a college football team. If that were to happen, Devin says, he'd like to study other cultures and geography. One of the best things about having played so much soccer so early is that he was able to travel all over the world. He'd like to build on those experiences in finding a college major and then possibly in working with kids, as a teacher or as a coach. "It all sounds cool to me," he says.

Devin knows all of this sounds a little strange, given how much he hated high school and how hard it was for him to focus and study. "If professors told me to do the assignments, I think I'd be doing them," he says. "I'm more street-smart than I was back then. I would understand that I would need to do the work. That I couldn't get away with not doing it." Devin says he's even willing to reconsider using medications to help with focus and concentration. Without a trace of self-importance, he says that he may even have "matured."

Beyond His Wildest Dreams

Is Devin ever upset or disappointed that he is different? "No," he says with great feeling. "Absolutely not. I knew what I wanted to be good at, and it had absolutely nothing to do with ADD." In fact, he says, because of ADD, he has more energy than most people, tires less easily on the field, and has a hyperfocus and drive that help him compete. ADD is the thing, he says, that makes him unstoppable on the soccer field and helps him have a life, as he says, that "goes beyond my wildest dreams."

Devin says that he wants kids to realize that even if they aren't cut out to be professional athletes, they should know that they are gifted at *something*. "Find something that you are good at and stick with it," he says. "Because when you have a talent that you know you have and your parents know you have—not something they pushed on you to get good at, but something that *you* love, that *you* have a lot of passion for—if you stick with it, it'll pay off in the long run. I'm positive."

Margaret Turano

Director, Marketing Communications,
Amicas

I always knew, deep down,
I was smart, smarter than
people thought I was. I knew
something was holding me
back. I just didn't know what
that thing was.

Date of Birth: October 9, 1966
Boston, Massachusetts

ASK MARGARET TURANO WHAT Mamie Eisenhower wore when her husband, Dwight D. Eisenhower, was inaugurated as president of the United States: "Sequins!" she snaps, laughing. How about Mary Todd Lincoln, wife of President Abraham Lincoln? "All black," Margaret says immediately. "She was in mourning." Margaret fell in love with inaugural ball gowns when, at ten, she visited the Smithsonian Institution in Washington, DC. "I was just fascinated with the first ladies of the United States," she says. "I can tell you what each one of them wore to the inauguration balls—right up through Roslyn Carter."

Margaret can't remember a time when she wasn't excited about design, decorating, and detail. She collected Madame Alexander dolls when she was young and still smiles when she thinks of her beloved dollhouse. "It was gorgeous,"

Margaret says. "I loved it." She spent hours organizing all the accessories. Its dining room table had miniature place servings for twelve. At Christmas, she would decorate the tiny trees around the dollhouse with real lights.

For a person who loves details, Margaret could never understand why she had such a hard time staying organized and keeping track of things. It took her years to figure out how to turn her passion for design into a successful career in business, where she could effectively keep track of details—lots and lots of details. The magic key was coming to terms with her ADD, and that didn't happen until several years ago.

Marketing Communications: Sequins and Business Savvy

Margaret works in marketing and public relations. She is now head of marketing communications for Amicas, a Boston-based company that designs computer software for radiology departments in hospitals. This software allows doctors to store their patients' medical images, including MRIs, CT scans, and digital versions of X-rays. With the push of a button, they can then send the images to computers around the world. "It's kind of like instant messaging between doctors," Margaret says.

Margaret's not kidding when she says she has to keep track of lots and lots of details. Her job is to talk with people in every part of the company, figuring out what each section needs to be able to sell the company's software to customers. To do this well—and Margaret does it very well—she has to know how to listen and respond intelligently to salespeople, customers, her company's business managers, doctors, engineers, and software designers. One of a few women in her particular field, Margaret encourages girls to think seriously about careers in business. Through the years, she's learned how to balance her appreciation of sequins with her savvy about business. "I don't act like a man," Margaret says, "but I know how to work with them and get the job done."

Margaret's skills have been particularly useful to her company. "When I started at this company, we were in a basement. We employed forty-five people. We had a phenomenal product—great technology—and a few customers. Not too many people knew who we were. Now we employ over three hundred people." It was part of Margaret's job to get out the word. "My team developed the look and feel, the imagery for the company," she says. Some of the ways they did this was by designing a Web site, creating packets of information, and making contact with journalists who could write articles about what the company had to offer.

Another part of Margaret's job is to go to conferences to explain to radiologists what the company's technology can do. At these conferences, she designs and has exhibits built so teams from the company can demonstrate the software to people from all over the world. For instance, this year, at a trade show in Chicago where sixty thousand radiologists gathered, she designed and staffed a booth with seventeen workstations, a theater presentation, and comfortable areas where visitors could relax and ask questions. Drawing on old skills she'd honed working on her dollhouse, Margaret made sure that the area was inviting, setting up comfortable couches and stocking food and drinks for visitors.

Not Knowing Why You're Struggling

As a kid, Margaret had never given a career a lot of thought. She was a terrific tennis player, a gifted pianist, and an enthusiastic performer in school plays and musicals. She figured she'd get married and have children, and that seemed like as much of a plan as she needed.

Growing up in London, Houston, and Los Angeles, Margaret found grade school a breeze but began to struggle in middle and high school, when focus and organization became a big part of getting good grades. In subjects that interested her—English, history, art history—she did well. It was a very different story in courses that didn't hold her interest. She remembers studying for more than twenty hours for a tenth-

grade biology test. "I think I got a seventeen," she says. Margaret's parents weren't too concerned about learning why their daughter was having such a hard time. They knew she was bright, but they thought that the reason she did poorly in some subjects was that she wasn't working hard enough and enjoyed making trouble.

After high school, Margaret headed to New England, entering Boston College, where she majored in English and psychology. "It was the same academic situation," she recalls. As in high school, Margaret did great in the subjects that interested her but did poorly in ones that did not.

When Margaret and her college boyfriend broke up, Margaret reevaluated her plans. She'd gotten a master's degree in education, but without a husband, she wasn't sure she would be happy living on a teacher's salary. Eager to try any kind of work, Margaret took a job in business by filling in for the secretary to the vice president of marketing in a biotechnology firm. She found that she loved marketing, and she was good at it. A permanent job opened up at the company as coordinator of marketing. Margaret spent three years in this job. She went on to take new marketing jobs in other companies, eventually sliding up into positions where she was in charge.

A Puzzle

Along the way, she was plagued by organizational disasters. For a person so tuned in to nuances and details, Margaret could not understand why she could not keep track of her own things, nor could she figure out why she could not reliably meet important deadlines. She was always losing her driver's license, her glasses, her wallet, and her keys. Once, she left her laptop on top of her car and drove off. Another time, she walked off a plane with the airline blanket wrapped around her shoulders—not her sweater, which she'd left behind. She'd frequently go to an ATM and leave her access

card behind. Friends joked that the trail of items she mis-
placed or lost were "Margaret droppings." Though she knew
there was truth in their observations, Margaret couldn't help
feeling awful about her inability to hang on to important
stuff.

It wasn't just in her personal life that Margaret suffered
from distractibility and disorganization. On the job, she'd
worry herself sick knowing that if she were to forget to register for trade shows on time, she'd prevent her company from
exhibiting. "If I failed to send a check, there wouldn't be a
show. It was my worst nightmare," she recalls.

Even though, on some level, Margaret knew she was
smart, these recurring incidents slowly left her feeling incom-
petent and stupid. She could see that she was great at certain
parts of her job, especially the parts that allowed her to be in-
ventive and creative. But the other parts, the parts that had
to do with keeping track of details, left her feeling terrified.
"At the time, it felt like it was just one befuddlement after another," she says. Some coworkers covered for her, helping to
make sure she didn't make mistakes. Others made fun of her.
"I laughed—I laughed right along with them," she remembers. "I had to. But it just killed me inside. I felt bad, like
I was just squeaking by."

An Answer: ADD

In 2002, the company Margaret was working for went out of
business. Unsure of what to do next, Margaret sought help
from a therapist, who realized in talking with her that

Margaret had ADD. Her first reaction was that "there was just no way." She took a test to confirm the therapist's diagnosis. "Talk about succeeding at a test!" she laughs. "I got an A plus on that one!" Margaret was thirty-five years old, facing, for the first time, the reality that she had ADD. "Maybe it was devastating for a few days," she says, "but then, suddenly, it was like finding out I had had a freckle my whole life in a certain spot. I just never knew it was there." Margaret decided that it wasn't so serious to have ADD. "Actually, it's *not* knowing that is so serious."

Within a week of diagnosis, Margaret tried medication. She said she might have been afraid, but she so completely trusted her therapist that she knew whether the medicine worked or not, she'd be OK. At first, Margaret said, the medication made her feel "tense" and "wired." After two months of trial and error, she at last found the right kind and dose of medication. Is her life different with medication? Absolutely, she says. "I can focus. I don't lose as much stuff. There are fewer 'Margaret droppings.'"

Strategies

One of the best things about knowing she has ADD, Margaret says, is that she doesn't have to spend so much time and energy finding lost things, dreading mistakes, and pretending it doesn't hurt to have colleagues pointing out her goofs. That's because these things just don't happen very often anymore, since Margaret has developed some effective coping strategies. For instance, now when she travels through airports, she clips her driver's license into a special see-through plastic rectangle on her belt so she doesn't lose it. She attaches her jewelry box to her suitcase with a string so she can't leave it behind in hotels. Instead of trying to keep up with one telephone headset, she has several—in her office, in her purse, in her car, in her home. "I have backups for everything. I can lose my keys, but I always know that I have another set at one friend's house or another's."

At work, Margaret now handles details more easily and stays efficient. She rarely misses deadlines because she uses special pop-up messages on her computer to remind herself of important upcoming dates and events. She also has a terrific assistant. When she prepares company budgets, she first color-codes everything for her own eyes to help her keep track of and proofread numbers and statistics. By the time she hands budgets to people in the finance department, she removes the colors and is able to turn in something she's proud of. "You've just got to learn to get over the obstacles," she says. "You can't do that, though, unless you know what you're dealing with."

"Before I knew I had ADD," Margaret says, "I was so frustrated all the time. I always knew, deep down, I was smart, smarter than people thought I was. I knew something was holding me back, keeping me from excelling. I just didn't know what that thing was."

Margaret has come to believe having ADD is a gift. It gives her more energy, a sense of passion for all that she does, and more creative ideas than she knows what to do with.

Knowing that she has ADD has given her a new understanding of herself, which has helped her career take off. "I wonder sometimes, if I had known I'd had ADD at fifteen . . ." Her voice trails off. "Well, maybe I could have been running a company. Hey!" she says. "I still *could* run a company. Someday I *will*!"

Richard Joseph Zienowicz, MD, FACS

Plastic and Reconstructive Surgeon

We have something powerful. We just need to learn how to use it to its full potential.

Date of Birth: October 6, 1954
Providence, Rhode Island

It was 7:30 p.m., November 1970, and Rick Zienowicz and his friends were in a car, rushing to get to a ball game. They went flying around a corner and smashed into a pole. The car did not have seat belts. Everyone was safe except for sixteen-year-old Rick, who had fractured his skull. A high school junior and basketball star at the time, Rick wound up in the hospital for a month. His balance returned to normal in six months, although he was dizzy for a year. Two things did not go away after the accident: (1) Rick became deaf in one ear, and (2) he fell permanently in love with medicine.

"I was exposed to a neurologist who took amazing care of me," he remembers. "His name was Michael Volpe." Dr. Volpe had swum across the Danube River to escape from Communist Hungary and train as a doctor in Vienna. When he immigrated to the United States, Dr. Volpe first worked for NASA. "He was the greatest guy. He was a caring, methodical, accomplished physician, and he took the time to talk to me. What a wonderful role model!"

Popular, Athletic, Premed . . . and Disorganized

Rick's parents knew he was bright but never insisted he excel. A fun-loving kid who did well in science, English, and history, Rick tended to be interested in a million things at once. It was hard for him to think or plan far ahead. "I was smart enough that my parents didn't have to push me," Rick recalls. "My parents never made me feel extraordinary. I mean, even though I was the most valuable player in the state for basketball when I was twelve, and I knew they were proud of me, they always had me feeling that I wasn't living up to my potential." Easily bored, Rick needed a lot of excitement, which he mostly got through playing the accordion, sports, and socializing. A popular athlete at the Catholic parochial schools he attended, Rick was voted "Winter Carnival King" in high school.

Rick headed off to college at Concordia University in Montreal, filled with a desire to explore the world, play basketball, and pursue a career in medicine. "I had a good time in college. The first year, I didn't study much," he says.

Declaring himself "premed," Rick took required classes, not all of which came easily. "My organizational skills were a problem. I thought I was more capable than a lot of people out there," he says, but he couldn't figure out how to show it on paper. In subjects that interested him, Rick did well. But his grades in physical chemistry and statistics, which he found unbelievably boring, for example, weren't great. With a lot of hard work and, as he says, "catching up," Rick managed to graduate cum laude (with honors) in biology.

Dr. Volpe stayed in touch with Rick after his recovery. During college summers Dr. Volpe encouraged Rick to try his hand at experimental science. One year, he got Rick to help researchers map a brain. Another year, he helped Rick get a job in a lab performing EEGs, tests that measure electrical impulses in the brain. Rick loved the hands-on work he was doing in the labs. The experiments made him absolutely sure he wanted to attend medical school after college to become a doctor.

Rick's MCAT Oops

To apply to medical school, college students have to sign up to take a special test—the Medical College Admission Test (MCAT). If they do well on this test, students have a good chance of becoming doctors. "I missed the deadline," Rick recalls, shaking his head. Too distracted by all the exciting things in his life—he helped run a dorm, a student center, and also played guitar—Rick neglected to register to take the MCAT. "I felt so stupid!" he says. Without MCAT scores, Rick could not even apply to find out if he could get into medical school. "I needed to remain attentive, to follow through," Rick says. He didn't know he had ADD, and he didn't know how to help himself pay attention to key steps that he needed to take. After so much special course work and extra studying, Rick still can't believe that he made such a careless, costly error. "I missed the detail that would've allowed me to achieve my goal."

Terribly frustrated, Rick returned to Providence and rented an apartment with a friend. He spent the next two years working in a psychiatric hospital, helping to chart the behaviors of patients needing serious mental health care—patients suffering from depression, manic depression, and schizophrenia, for example. "I had never spent time with these kinds of people before," Rick says. "I watched them, wrote up my daily observations, played games with them, talked with them. I loved it, and I was really good at it." Doctors at the psychiatric hospital encouraged Rick to apply to medical school. "I had a choice. I had the option of taking the MCAT and waiting a year and a half to find out if I could get into a medical school here in the United States, or I could go to Mexico. That sounded faster."

Medical School and Surgery

Rick liked the idea of going to Mexico. "I love languages, and I love challenges!" he says, remembering his preparations for Mexico. "I took some Spanish and loved it," Rick says. Rick entered medical school in Guadalajara with three hundred other students. He married his girlfriend from Providence, and she moved to Mexico to be with him. At the end of his second year, he was one of the top five students in his class. "I went down to Guadalajara and had never worked so hard before. *Everything* was in Spanish—all the technical information and medical terms—*everything.*"

After two years in Mexico, Rick was accepted into the third year of medical school at Brown University, an Ivy League school in his hometown of Providence. The third year of medical school is when students get a chance to practice a variety of medical specialties. Even though Rick had had experience in neurology with Dr. Volpe and psychiatry at the psychiatric hospital, he decided he was more interested in something that would allow him to be physically active. Surgery excited Rick from the moment he practiced dissection (cutting open bodies to study them). "I dissected cats, frogs. I reconstructed skeletons. I was fascinated." When it came time to make a decision, to Rick, it was a no-brainer. "With neurology and psychiatry, there was too much talking. So, I just knew right away," he says. "Surgery."

At Brown, Rick's teachers recognized his talent for surgery. They recommended him for a five-year course in general surgery at the University of Massachusetts. "Surgery is all about finding problems and fixing them. Ninety-nine percent of the time, people are better after I'm done than when I started." Rick noticed that he was especially good at surgery because he thought and worked so quickly. "I got frustrated when I saw people missing things I thought were obvious," he says. "They weren't moving at lightning speed."

Plastic and Reconstructive Surgery

Rick followed his initial rounds of general surgery with two years of instruction in plastic surgery at the Cleveland Clinic and two more years of training in hand microsurgery at Massachusetts General Hospital in Boston. When he wasn't working, Rick was training to compete in triathlons. He knew he needed exceptional stamina to get through what were sometimes 120-hour workweeks. While other doctors-in-training strained under the workload, Rick says he sailed through because he simply had more energy than almost everyone he knew.

To Rick, nothing is better than plastic and reconstructive surgery. "There's an incredible variety," he says. "There's just nothing in medicine that gives you as many potential solutions to different problems." In addition, he says, he gets to use what he calls "3-D thinking." "I'm rebuilding pieces of the body from scratch," he says. "That requires endless creativity." Rick takes great satisfaction from being able to make people feel good about how they look. Whether he's making a new breast for a woman who has had breast cancer, reattaching fingers for people who've lost the use of their hands in accidents, or repairing facial deformities on children with birth defects, Rick is never bored and always gratified when he's done a good job. These days, he sees patients in his office one day a week and operates the other four days a week, alternating between reconstructive and plastic surgery.

When Brown University offered him a job on its medical school faculty to teach plastic and reconstructive surgery,

Rick returned to Providence. Rick's marriage had ended in Cleveland. His ex-wife had resettled with their two daughters in Providence. "I wanted to be near them," he says. Rick met his second wife when he was working in Boston. A dancer and pediatric anesthesiologist, she specializes in giving children medicines to make them sleep when they are having surgery. "She's a phenomenally talented woman," Rick says. "And like me, she uses strenuous exercise to help stay focused."

ADD: My Heart Leapt for Joy

In the early 1990s, Rick had taken his daughters on a trip to Florida to visit his mother when he read an article about ADD in the newspaper. "I called my wife, and I said, 'This is unbelievable! This is me!'" He made an appointment to meet with a doctor, who asked him all sorts of questions about focus, organization, boredom, and attention. The doctor agreed that Rick had ADD. "My heart leaped for joy," Rick says. "It was the single most important revelation in my life— unquestionably. To put a label on something you've *never* been able to understand . . . to understand, all of a sudden . . . I just felt so much better about myself." With the diagnosis, Rick understood why he could pull 120-hour workweeks without crumbling but couldn't register for the MCAT on time. And he wasn't mad at himself anymore. "ADD is one of my genetic gifts," he says. "Because it *is* a gift. The advantages far exceed the disadvantages. With medicine, the bad parts can be controlled."

I Wish More People Got Medicines

The doctor suggested that Rick try Ritalin. Rick says that he used the medication to help him do things that were hard for him. He didn't need Ritalin for surgery. "It doesn't make any difference in that part of my life at all, because in the operating room, I hyperfocus." Ritalin, he says, "helped me do the stuff that I hate," such as filling out insurance forms and writing papers. Recently, Rick transitioned off Ritalin. He finds that it has served its purpose, but now a little caffeine is sufficient.

Once Rick understood ADD, he suspected his daughters from his first marriage had it as well. He took them to a doctor, who diagnosed them and prescribed stimulants. "Both of my kids would have struggled to finish high school without medication," he says. Rick worries that too many people with undiagnosed ADD do things like drink alcohol or take illegal drugs to help them cope with symptoms they can't control. "I wish more people got medicines for ADD," he says.

Many people with ADD suffer from feelings of inadequacy and low self-esteem, Rick says, and they don't think they'll ever measure up—even when they are succeeding. "We have something powerful," he says of people with ADD. "We just need to learn how to use it to its full potential."

SEELAN PARAMANANDAM MANICKAM

Musician

Friends say I'm like a pit bull. I bite, and I just don't let go.

Date of Birth: April 17, 1971
Boston, Massachusetts

WHAT DO YOU DO WHEN YOU FIND THE THING YOU LOVE—the thing you do better than most everyone in the world—and your parents shout, "NO!" That was Seelan Manickam's question after he told his parents in the ninth grade that he wanted to become a professional trumpeter. "I mean, they loved music," Seelan says, "but definitely not for a career." Growing up in a small town in western Canada as the only son of immigrants, Seelan learned at an early age that it was important to work hard and do well in school. But the only thing he wanted to work hard at was trumpet, and he never did very well in school. "Where I grew up, nobody thought of music as anything serious," he says. "It was just for fun." So, how did Seelan become a professional trumpeter? "Friends say I'm like a pit bull," he laughs. "I bite, and I just don't let go."

Seelan surely got his stubbornness from his parents, no strangers to hard times and struggle. Born on the island of Sri Lanka, south of India, his father (a teacher) and mother moved to India to escape civil war and raise a family. They eventually moved to Canada to join friends and find work, settling in Williams Lake, a small town in the northern part of British Columbia. Seelan remembers his dad tirelessly writing letters, applying for teaching jobs, and working in a lumber mill to make ends meet. "He's the kind of guy who does what needs to be done," Seelan says with great admiration.

Definitely "Hyperactive"

The stubbornness that prevented Seelan's dad from giving up hope made him hard to have as a dad. It was, Seelan explains, a tough match—a father who was a perfectionist educator and a son who mostly hated school, where teachers complained he talked too much, couldn't sit still, and bothered other students. Seelan struggled with math. He loved to read, but he had a hard time organizing his thoughts and writing them down. This made Seelan's parents angry—especially Seelan's father—who believed that education was the key to success.

Despite his difficulties, Seelan made relatively good grades until junior high. There, Seelan's grades fell. His teachers sent him to see the school guidance counselor. She sent Seelan to the nurse for tests. "I got called back to the counselor's office. 'We think you're definitely hyperactive—that was the word they used for ADD back then," he says. The idea that Seelan had ADD, that he was, in his parents' terms, "hyper," horrified Seelan's parents. They would not believe that their son needed help, especially since until then, he had done well in school. What they didn't know was that bright kids with ADD often have a harder time in middle school and junior high, when assignments get more complicated and the deadlines start coming fast and furious.

Seelan's parents hadn't a clue as to what to make of the school's diagnosis. "A 'mental defect' was *not* allowed," Seelan says. "They thought there should be *no* excuse for my behavior. It just didn't matter that there might be an explanation. They just said, 'You need to calm down.'" But Seelan couldn't calm down on his own. And school did not get any easier.

Amazing Grace

There was, meanwhile, one thing he could do best. Two weeks before Seelan had started fourth grade, every student got a chance to pick a band instrument. Seelan doesn't know why, but he instantly wanted to play the trumpet. His parents

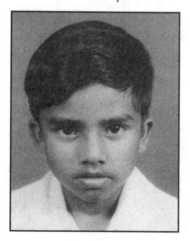

rented an old trumpet and bought him a music book for the year. Within a week, Seelan had memorized the fingerings from the back of the trumpet book. A week later, he played "Amazing Grace" in front of everyone at church.

Trumpet, Seelan says, instantly became "his thing." He practiced an hour a day, and soon, he was known at school as the best trumpeter in his grade. He practiced because he loved the feel of making music. He also worked hard, he says, because he needed to be really good at *something*.

While Seelan's parents were glad he'd found the trumpet, they still expected him to do great at school. Without help to cope with ADD, Seelan continued to get into trouble. When he made bad grades or fought at school, his parents would ground him, prevent him from playing team sports, or take away TV time. "They blamed me," Seelan remembers. "In their minds, hyperactivity wasn't a medical condition." Working in the lumber mill, teaching science courses in community college, and substitute teaching, Seelan's dad was exhausted from holding down three jobs and had little patience for what he saw as Seelan's unnecessary troublemaking. "My dad would hit me if I was bad," Seelan remembers. "I was scared of my father—maybe even up until college."

To some kids with ADD, Seelan's experiences will sound awfully familiar. Parents of kids with ADD often don't understand that without extra support in organization and planning, without plenty of time to move around and play sports, and, in many cases, without medication, their children won't be able to make good grades and behave well at school and at home. Not knowing that there are real things that can make a big difference, parents may yell a lot and even, in frustration, hit their children. This is tough on kids with ADD, who may want to do well but don't know how to make things better. As a result, kids may get angry with teachers and parents and, worst of all, may get sad and lose faith in themselves.

Never Giving Up

Showing the same determination his father demonstrated in his search for work, Seelan did not give up. A few teachers at school recognized Seelan's intelligence and worked hard to help him learn. The good ones, he says, allowed him to be imaginative. They sat him near the front of the class. Best, he says, they helped him find ways to work hard at things he didn't do well and did not make him feel like a failure in the process.

And then, Seelan says, there were the music teachers. They loved Seelan. Sure, Seelan talked out of turn in band and didn't behave particularly well, but when he played his trumpet, the sound was true and clear and *alive*. His seventh-grade teacher was so impressed with Seelan's musical abilities that he got him to play solos for a visiting professional trumpeter. "He gave me a private lesson after band," Seelan recalls, grinning. "He gave me his card and said, 'Come study with me after high school.'" Seelan was thrilled. He told his parents. His dad, Seelan says, was proud but declared that playing trumpet was not what he wanted his son to do. The teacher convinced Seelan's parents that their son's gifts were so extraordinary that they merited the purchase of an $800 trumpet. "It was a real turning point," Seelan says.

By ninth grade, Seelan knew that he wanted to be a professional musician. As in every other part of his life, he hated the tedious bits, especially practicing scales and finger exercises. Half an hour of these seemed like an eternity. He got bored. He had trouble focusing. He fidgeted. He couldn't keep track of the time. His mother nagged him. "I was frustrated with myself," Seelan says. But Seelan loved trumpet so much that he kept going. By tenth grade, he was practicing two hours a day. His trumpet teacher told him that if he wanted to be a pro, he'd need to study piano and music theory. Though his parents initially refused, in the end, they allowed Seelan to work with his little sister's teacher, Wendy Bernier, a woman he describes as "beautiful—just a terrific musician."

Seelan's school held a yearly competition for musicians, starting in seventh grade. "I won every single year," Seelan says. The winner would get recommended to go on to a regional festival. The town expected the winner's family to pay for the trip. Seelan's parents never had the money to send him, so the school always advanced another student. Finally, when Seelan was a junior in high school, his teacher, Wendy, threw a fit. "If you don't send Seelan," she said, "then nobody is going." The school scraped together the money, and Seelan finally got to attend.

A Pretty Amazing Musician

Even as they witnessed their son's victories, Seelan's parents did not want him to continue music studies in college. As for Seelan, he had had enough school. Once again, Wendy stepped in. "She said I *had* to have a degree," Seelan recalls. She showed Seelan how to apply to various programs. The University of

85

Victoria, where his older sister was studying, invited Seelan to audition. After his audition and interview, Seelan went with the head of the music school to find his parents. "'You've got a pretty amazing musician, there,'" the music school head said. "I mean, there I was, from this small lumber town. My grades were terrible. I barely had a C+ average. I'd almost failed math, had failed computer science, and had withdrawn from chemistry. I just didn't think I would get in."

When the acceptance letter came to his high school, Seelan raced to his favorite teacher's class. He had won a scholarship. "She grabbed the letter and screamed!" Seelan then raced home to tell his mother. "She was upset with me that I'd left school." Were his parents proud? Seelan says that he's sure they were. They certainly didn't want him having to work in the lumber mill, and a college degree, they hoped, would make a big difference. But they didn't think Seelan would ever be able to support himself playing trumpet, with or without a college degree.

College: Feeling Like a Joke

The same problems that had plagued him in high school stayed with Seelan in college. With a major in music performance, Seelan continued to get As in every course in trumpet playing. Since he had never learned to come to terms with having ADD and had never learned the organizational skills he needed to manage his schoolwork, Seelan continued to struggle in the subjects that didn't come easily. Young and irresponsible, he fell into a pattern of skipping classes, not turning in assignments, and forgetting to sign up for required courses. His grades were so bad that he lost his scholarship. Although they were fed up with what they viewed as their son's recklessness, Seelan's parents agreed to pay his tuition.

Through all of this, Seelan felt like a joke. "People said, 'He's never going to make it,'" Seelan remembers. And for a while, Seelan wasn't sure he would make it. At the end of his four years of college, he realized he wouldn't have enough credits to graduate. Seelan still had to pass an English course and pass an exam in musical keyboarding. His big sister helped him with the English essays, but he still had the keyboard proficiency class to pass. Just weeks before the semester was ending, Seelan learned that, rather than sitting to take a written test, he could choose to *play* the keyboard exam. "I crammed for two weeks," he remembers. "I nailed it." After six long years, Seelan graduated from college with a degree in music performance. Is he glad that he stuck it out? "I'm glad now, but I sure wasn't at the time."

Graduate School: Getting His Act Together

Seelan's college professors told him that if he wanted to continue as a professional musician, he would need to get a graduate degree. The thought of more school made his stomach ache. Seelan learned about performance-based programs—conservatories, or music schools—where students mostly just play their instruments all day and all night long. This, he thought, was something he might be able to handle. After interviewing in San Francisco and Boston, Seelan accepted a full scholarship to the Boston Conservatory. He arrived with a steamer trunk full of gear in the fall of 1995, ready to make a fresh start.

Even though he began taking lessons, practicing, and participating in an ensemble, Seelan was plagued with worries about failure, and he still had problems meeting deadlines and following through, especially with written work. After he took a summer off to mountain bike and think, Seelan grew up a bit, realizing that even though he had finally gotten himself to the place he wanted to be, he had never learned how to focus and get organized. Ready to learn the skills he would need to succeed, he finally took some classes that gave him tools he needed to get his act together.

"I grew up and remade myself," he says. "In a last-ditch attempt to make it as a trumpeter, I turned into 'the serious guy.' I was practicing four to five hours a day, and I was *really focused.*"

The dean of the conservatory noticed Seelan's dramatically different approach to his work. He reached out to Seelan and explained that to earn his master's degree in trumpet performance, Seelan could do a project instead of a written thesis. Seelan was overjoyed. He decided to teach a special class in the basics of brass playing for high school beginners. He had the class videotaped and submitted the tape as his thesis. Seelan passed with flying colors. "That degree meant more to me than anything," he says, beaming. "I was so proud of this degree. I was *proud* of myself."

All the Good Things

The degree, Seelan says, was his ticket to all the good things he had always wanted. Out of school and able to earn a living, Seelan married his girlfriend and had a child. He has made enough of a name for himself that he's been invited to work as a guest performer with orchestras throughout New England and parts of Canada. He formed an ensemble, which he named Bala Brass. *Bala* is a concept of five strengths (conviction, persistence, mindfulness, concentration, and discernment), all of which Seelan had to work on to become a professional musician. Bala Brass has made a CD and has been invited to perform all over the world. Using his humor and insights into children, Seelan is the musical director at a private boys' high school in Massachusetts. He also teaches trumpet to students privately.

Sweetest of all to Seelan was a recent invitation to return home to Williams Lake to deliver a speech at a teachers' conference about the importance of art and music in schools. Seelan decided he didn't want to give a talk. "I was one of those kids who *loved* music, and I wanted to show what level it can go to. I wanted to give them proof of this." Seelan played a forty-minute concert to an audience in his hometown school district made up, in part, of family and his own former teachers. Afterward, Seelan's high school math teacher came up to say hello. He remembered that he'd told Seelan that he would "never amount to anything." Not an easy thing to hear, Seelan says, after he'd just played out his heart and soul. "But this is what this teacher said to me," Seelan says. "'You've proven me wrong for the first time.'"

From that moment on, Seelan says, his parents became "extremely supportive." True, they'd given him money for school and rent over the years, Seelan says, but they had never given him respect. At last, his dad understood that the trumpet had really given Seelan a life and a career.

SHARON WOHLMUTH

Photographer

Really understand what's going on in your brain.

Date of Birth: September 25, 1946
Philadelphia, Pennsylvania

WHEN SHARON WOHLMUTH WAS A CHILD growing up in Bristol, Connecticut, her parents took her to a specialist who gave her some tests to see how well she learned. She remembers the sound of the workers using drills outside the room. She still remembers food stuck in the teeth of the man giving her the tests.

When it was time for Sharon to apply to college, she needed to take another test—the Scholastic Aptitude Test, or SAT. Although she recalls liking some parts of the test, especially the analogies, once again it was sights, sounds, and smells that impressed her. The SAT was given in a cafeteria. She found herself distracted by the smell of food. There was also a big rainstorm. "The rain was beating against the windows so hard," she says, "I spent most of my time staring outside."

In both cases, Sharon was so busy sensing her surroundings that she couldn't focus on what she needed to be doing: answering the test questions. Neither Sharon's parents nor Sharon knew that her ability to pick up on all those details—those sights and smells and sounds—was causing the very real problems that kept her from doing well in school. They also did not know that this ability would help Sharon to become a photographer who would win a Pulitzer Prize, one of the most prestigious awards for creative work in the United States, and create best-selling books.

A Very Lovely Girl

No one knew that Sharon had ADD. Back in the 1950s and 1960s, when Sharon was growing up, parents and teachers labeled kids "dumb" who were easily distracted and had a hard time focusing their attention. Even though Sharon didn't do badly on either set of tests, she came away feeling stupid. "My parents never told me what the results were," Sharon remembers of the first set of tests. "Later on, I found out I did pretty well. But what they told me was that I was a very lovely girl with a wonderful personality and that I would make a wonderful mother."

Although Sharon was glad to know her parents thought she was "lovely," she desperately wanted them to think of her as smart and capable. Her family prized education and academic achievement. Most of the boys in her parents' families had gone to Yale, a prestigious Ivy League university. Sharon's father wanted her to prepare for a similar kind of education, so he insisted she be tutored in Latin and German.

No Diagnosis, No Strategies

Since her parents and teachers didn't know about ADD, they couldn't help Sharon figure out how to focus better. For example, she always did her homework at the dining room table—not the best strategy for someone with ADD who wants to study and is easily distracted. "It was the worst place I could have done it," she says. "The newspaper was there, my mother would be on the telephone talking, there were all the smells of what she was cooking, and across the table my dad would be teaching my sister chess."

Without any other changes in the way Sharon was expected to learn and without medication, Sharon continued to have a hard time with most subjects, except for English, and she worried constantly that she was disappointing her parents, especially her father. He was, she says, frustrated by her inabil-

ity to learn things he thought she needed to know for college, especially math and foreign languages.

Sharon's childhood wasn't all struggle and unhappiness. She adored being outdoors, climbing trees, and riding her bike. There were plenty of kids to play with in her neighborhood, and she regularly walked to school with a group of girls. In the summer, she would go to the beach, where her family met up with aunts, uncles, and cousins. Interested in boys by high school, Sharon participated in the social whirl of Jewish youth organizations, going to Hebrew school and dances, where she made friends and had fun. "It was a long, sweet childhood," she says, "except when it came to school."

The Curse and Blessing of Shorthand

Sharon's parents concluded that if she wasn't a strong student, she needed to plan on getting married. There was no sense that her life might go in other directions, that there might be other possibilities for her. While all her friends got ready to go to fancy women's colleges, Sharon headed for Fisher Junior College outside Boston. She was to study to become a secretary, which her parents told her she could drop as soon as she found a suitable man to marry. At Fisher, she did well at accounting, found typing hard, and was lost when it came to shorthand, which is a way to write speech as fast as it is spoken. "I *hated* shorthand," Sharon says. "I couldn't even learn it. I must have really tried, but I could not do it."

About the same time that Sharon was having such a hard time with shorthand, she met a boy along the Charles River who had a ten-speed bike. Behaving impulsively (which can happen a lot when you have ADD), Sharon borrowed the bike and went riding off. "I was wearing a skirt, and I got on the bike in the skirt. I was flying along. It was so great. Suddenly, there were these marble steps, and I was looking for foot brakes, but there were hand brakes!" Sharon remembers. Unable to stop the bike, Sharon went tumbling down the stairs on the bike, fell, and lost her two front teeth. When she returned to college from the emergency room, the woman in charge of her dormitory spoke roughly to her. "You deserve this!" the woman said.

When the people in charge of Fisher College found out about the accident, and when they realized Sharon was failing shorthand, they asked her to leave. Sharon's parents came to pick her up. She remembers two things about that day. She remembers a tremendous sense of shame and embarrassment. She also remembers that as she was putting a suitcase in her parents' car, a girl whispered, "You're so lucky," in Sharon's ear. Sharon couldn't have known then how true those words would turn out to be.

Art: My Life Began

After her time at Fisher, she first worked in the Bristol public library and then in a travel agency. An airline threw a bash in Hartford for people in the travel business, and at her mother's urging, Sharon got dressed up and went. "I met a charming, handsome, much older man there," she says. "When I got home, my parents were waiting. I told them, 'I think I met the man I'm going to marry.'" As soon as she told her parents that he was Jewish, had earned a degree from the University of Pennsylvania, and had a good business, they were thrilled. Within six months, the two had married, and Sharon moved to Philadelphia to be with him.

At first, Sharon enjoyed being married. In Philadelphia, Sharon and her husband lived on the twenty-sixth floor of an apartment building. Because her husband had a travel business, they took trips all the time. She saw parts of the world she'd only ever imagined. Even with the high-rise apartment and the travel, Sharon soon became restless and bored. The second year she was married, she started taking classes at the University of Pennsylvania as a part-time student. Sharon decided she wanted to go to art school. She had taken classes in painting and drawing for a few years when she was a girl, and she had loved them. It had never occurred to her before that she might study art full-time. With her husband's blessing, she enrolled in Moore College of Art and Design, an art school for women. "The moment I walked in that door," she says, "my life began."

Like so many people with ADD, Sharon blossomed when a teacher took special interest in her. Sharon launched into painting and then switched to photography. A teacher looked at Sharon's work and exclaimed, "God! This is *fantastic!*" Sharon was completely surprised. "It is?" she asked. "I never believed in myself," Sharon says. Her teacher gave her the confidence to keep going. Sharon would stay late at school working on projects, even after the art buildings were locked. "The kids who lived in the dorm helped me jump out of the window at two o'clock in the morning."

The more involved she got in school, the more Sharon realized that she and her husband were living in different worlds. It was 1966, a time when young people were experimenting with different ideas and ways of living. "I would walk

to the square, and there was a whole new world outside—
hippies, people in blue jeans. There I was, wearing sophisti-
cated 'outfits.' Inside, I was dying." Though she and her
husband cared about each other, they wanted different
things. Sharon's father died that year—1973—and though
this made Sharon very sad, she felt freed from the weight of
his judgment and able in new ways to follow her own path.
She and her husband ended their marriage that year.

Photojournalism

Once Sharon had graduated, in 1975, she found a small apartment and went to work as a photographer for the *Philadelphia
Inquirer*. "Working at the newspaper, it was the perfect job for
me," she says. Instead of being slowed down or thrown off
course by the details—the sights, sounds, and smells that
routinely flooded her mind—Sharon found that they were
the things that made her take better photographs than other
people.

"The details and descriptions—I turned that around. I
used them for my benefit. I saw that I had real gifts that other
people didn't have," she says. "If I could use them and harness
them in a way that worked for me, then they were a true benefit." Her impulsivity came in handy when she needed to act
quickly to get a great shot, whether that meant having the
split-second timing to push the camera's buttons, not being
afraid to take risks and jump over train tracks to find the
right angle, or not thinking before blurting out questions
about people's personal lives.

"I wasn't a struggling student anymore. I didn't have to worry about my grades," she says. "I was doing something that I totally loved, and I was respected." During the twenty-one years she worked at the *Inquirer*, Sharon won all sorts of prizes, including a Pulitzer Prize for group work on a story about a hazardous spill at a nuclear power plant called Three Mile Island.

Sisters

Everything was going great for Sharon. She loved her job. She met a man who appreciated all of her strengths and accepted her weaknesses. Then her mother got seriously ill. For eight years, she traveled between Philadelphia and her mother's home in Bristol so that she could help her younger sister take care of their mom. Even though it was tiring to work at the newspaper, stay in touch with her boyfriend, and help care for her mother, Sharon was glad to be close enough to help out. Though her mother died, Sharon had a chance to get to know her sister as an adult and to test the bond with her boyfriend, whom she later married.

The conversations she had with her sister during their mother's illness inspired Sharon to produce a book, *Sisters*, which is a collection of photographs and stories about the relationships sisters form. The book was so popular that it quickly sold out in stores. It was on the *New York Times* best-seller list for sixty-three weeks. Sharon took a year's leave of absence from the newspaper to promote *Sisters*. When the book hit number two on the *Times* best-seller list, her publisher offered her a contract to create two more books, *Mothers and*

Daughters and *Best Friends*. Sharon decided to leave the newspaper to work full-time taking photographs for books.

ADD: Don't I Do All of This?

Sharon still did not know that she had ADD. From time to time at the newspaper, she would read stories about children and ADD. "That was the beginning of having an inkling about ADD, but I thought it was only about kids." After she'd decided to leave the newspaper, she and her husband took a trip to the beach. As she was packing, she threw a book about ADD someone had sent her into her suitcase. Sitting on the beach, reading the book, she scanned the list of symptoms. "I sat up. I started screaming, 'These are the ten signs, and don't I do *all* of this? Oh, my God! This is *me*.'" When she got home, Sharon went to a doctor who diagnosed her as having ADD and prescribed Ritalin for her to take. She also found an ADD coach. "I felt like this whole mystery was solved. It was like pieces of a puzzle coming together." She wished her father had still been alive so that she could have talked to him. "I would have told him, 'I have ADD, and this is why you yelled at me all the time.'"

Now that she knows she has ADD, Sharon asks for help on the things that are hard for her. She never tries to work when there is music playing or noise around. Sharon makes sure that she doesn't try to take on too many projects at once; otherwise, she gets distracted and never finishes anything. She has an assistant who helps keep track of important papers and bills. Sharon uses colored circles on her calendar to help remind her what she needs to do. She's also learned to use a good filing system.

Sharon doesn't take Ritalin when she's photographing, because when she's working with a camera, she is hyperfocused. She takes her medicine when she needs to be organized and focused while doing things that are hard for her. If she's cleaning her office or wanting to write a speech, she takes a pill. "I first tried it five or six years ago," she says of the medicine. "I was nervous about taking it—and also excited. I remember swallowing it and thinking, 'What's going to happen?' It was profound. I opened all my mail. I thought, 'Oh, my God! This is astounding!'"

Understand What's Going On in Your Brain

Sharon hopes that now that doctors, parents, and teachers know so much more about ADD, they can diagnose kids early and spare them the kind of misery she endured. Her advice to kids is that they not settle for taking a pill, alone, to deal with their ADD. "Really understand what's going on in your brain," she says. "That's important because then you can ask for extra help and find your special talents."

Even though she struggled for so many years without knowing why, Sharon says she feels—as the girl told her when she was packing up to leave Fisher College—that she is lucky. "God forbid if I had passed shorthand. Then what would have happened? I don't even want to imagine!"

Harbhajan Singh Khalsa

Yogic Healer

Don't say, "I'm not good enough," or allow labels to define who you are or what you do.

Date of Birth: September 13, 1950
Taos, New Mexico

HARBHAJAN SINGH KHALSA SITS IN A CHAIR holding himself gently upright. Gaze softened, white turban slightly moving, Harbhajan (har-budg/-in) chants in a descending scale: "Sa-ta-na-ma. Sa-ta-na-ma." In time with his words, he gently touches alternating fingers to thumbs. This, he has explained earlier, is a meditation that, if done regularly before bedtime, helps balance and calm the brain. When he has finished his cycle of repetitions, he breathes deeply and smiles, the creases around his eyes fanning out in arcs of delight. Harbhajan has a way of practicing that makes meditation look fun. Not a medical doctor, Harbhajan is nonetheless a healer, a person devoted to helping people lessen pain in their bodies and minds. When Harbhajan talks about ADD, he chooses terms such as "spirit," "soul," and "brain calibration." Rather than using medicines, he teaches patients to practice meditation and yoga, which, he counsels, will help them live well with their difficulties. He knows this firsthand. He has used yoga and meditation for nearly thirty years to manage his own symptoms of ADD.

A yogic healer and ski instructor in Taos, New Mexico, Harbhajan was born Martin Luther Hungerford III. He changed his name when he was twenty-six after becoming a student of Yogi Bhajan, the founder of the American branch of the Indian-based Sikh Dharma (or "way of life"). To learn how Harbhajan came to change his name and become a Sikh healer is to understand how one person creatively came to terms with feelings of despair and inadequacy, much of which came from not understanding that he had ADD.

Kept Back in School

Growing up in Hamden, Connecticut, Harbhajan always struggled in school. "I stayed back in second and fifth grade," he says. "I just could not focus in school. I had problems lis-

tening and reading." Harbhajan did not know he was dyslexic or that he had ADD until he was in his forties. Not knowing why so much of school was hard, Harbhajan says he "shut down" and felt really awful about himself. "It was horrible to be kept back. It was degrading. I was so devastated emotionally about staying back in school that I thought about not being here—about suicide. I knew if I didn't perform well in school, I would be held back again, and I couldn't bear to stay back again. I was so self-conscious. There was just too much pain."

Even as school administrators pushed Harbhajan into lower-level classes and machine shop, he knew he was great at two things: math and recess. In general, he says, math came easily, which didn't make sense if, as people at school said, he wasn't smart. "I was *always* good with numbers." Later, in high school, he got As and Bs even in complicated math classes such as calculus.

Sports: Something to Calm Me Down

Harbhajan might have struggled in the classroom, but outdoors, it was a different story. "At recess, I was *the best*," he says. "I outperformed everyone in class. Like in kickball—I always kicked the ball the farthest." As he grew older, that love of recess developed into a love of sports. Harbhajan ran indoor track and played football and baseball. In track one year, he set an indoor state record for running the three-hundred-yard dash. Another year, he made the all-state team in football as a defensive back and won a leadership award in sports.

Harbhajan noticed that the more time he spent on sports, the better he did in school. He remembers practicing all year round. "It helped me do well in school," he says. "I needed something to calm me down." Though he wouldn't know until many years later how to describe what was happening to him, these days, Harbhajan says that exercise "balanced" his brain.

It took Harbhajan another ten years before he began to grasp the relationship between his body and his mind. During that decade he attended junior college and earned a degree in business and accounting—something that involved a lot of math and numbers. Harbhajan's father wanted him to use the degree to join the family business, Hungerford, Inc., a well-drilling company. "My dad wanted me to please him," Harbhajan recalls, "but he kept treating me like a child." Harbhajan had worked part-time for his dad from the time he was eight years old until he finished high school. "I didn't want any part of the business," he says. "My dad was really disappointed."

From a Hippie Lifestyle
to a Holy Life Choice

In college, lots of the students were experimenting with drugs. A self-described "clean-cut jock," Harbhajan at first steered clear of the hippie lifestyle that became popular in the late 1960s. After a while, though, Harbhajan tried smoking marijuana. He started thinking about and looking at the world in different ways. For four months in 1972, with sixty dollars in his pocket, Harbhajan hitchhiked around the country. "I was living in the moment!" he says, his eyes sparkling, his long beard rippling as he laughs. "Wow!"

After his travels, Harbhajan landed on Cape Cod, where he worked as a carpenter. By 1973, he had learned how to meditate and practice yoga. In 1974, he learned of Yogi Bhajan's teachings. Taking illegal drugs, Yogi Bhajan taught, is a terrible idea because they give a false sense of freedom and well-being. If people aren't relaxed and happy, the Yogi taught, they need to make important changes in their lives. To Yogi Bhajan, the best way to change is to practice yoga and meditation. He taught his students to pursue "3HO"—healthiness, happiness, and holiness. Yogi Bhajan also encouraged his students to work hard and start businesses.

Yoga and the Sikh Dharma

All of this made sense to Harbhajan. He especially liked what Yogi Bhajan had to say about using yoga to rebuild and balance the nervous system—the part of the body that controls anxiety, impulsivity, and other symptoms of ADD. Even more than track and football did, yoga helped Harbhajan with what he describes as "brain calibration." Scientists have been researching the ways that particular kinds of exercises calm and regulate the brain, the master control of the central nervous system. Perhaps scientists find it amazing that yoga helps ADD, but those, like Harbhajan, who engage in rigorous, daily yoga practice aren't surprised in the least. "The ancients knew what they were doing," Harbhajan says. "Yoga helped me focus, helped me keep my attention on *one* thing instead of jumping all over the place. I wasn't spacing out anymore." Not a fan of medications such as Ritalin, Harbhajan believes it is possible, by training the brain through specific yoga exercises, to alleviate symptoms of ADD by sending nerve signals from different parts of the body that put both halves of the brain in sync.

In 1976, when Harbhajan was twenty-six, he changed his name and became a Sikh, vowing to wear special clothing and committing himself to prayer, yoga, and a vegetarian diet. In addition, he followed Sikh practice and entered into an arranged marriage with his wife, Raj Inder Khalsa. By then, his parents had divorced, and his mother, without influence from her son, had chosen to follow Sikh teachings as well. Becoming a Sikh brought Harbhajan "into a new, spiritual family," he says. "It also allowed me to balance my mind, body, and spirit. It made me *whole*. It transformed my life. I would not be here, in this body, without it."

Working hard has always been an important part of Harbhajan's commitment to the Sikh dharma. Initially, Harbhajan joined an ashram, or closed community, outside of Boston, where he could live with others who were practicing yoga and following Sikh teachings. In 1978, he moved to San Diego, an important center of Sikh life, where he ran a plumbing business with Vikram Singh Khalsa, formerly known as Victor Briggs. Vikram had been a lead guitarist for the 1960s rock band the Animals and had cowritten "Sky Pilot," an angry song protesting America's involvement in the war in Vietnam. Like Harbhajan, Vikram took Yogi Bhajan as his teacher and became a Sikh. Together, the two worked with eight employees building restaurants. By the time Harbhajan was turning thirty-six, he was ready to do something else. He worked for and ran a variety of Sikh-owned businesses in areas including insurance, water purification, and organizational planning, but he still wasn't satisfied with his work.

A Healer

Four years later, in 1990, when he turned forty, Harbhajan decided he was ready to go back to school. With plenty of experience using his hands as a carpenter and construction worker, he chose to use his hands to heal. He started his training in acupuncture, a Chinese method of healing relying on puncturing the body with needles in precise spots to reduce pain and bring about good health. Although he came close to completing the acupuncture training, Harbhajan decided that he would change his focus slightly, becoming certified to perform special kinds of healing massage and touch. "I learned to deal with the subtleties and energies of the body," Harbhajan says, "to open up the body and give it space to heal. I focused on blood flow, the nervous system, and emotional work through the brain."

At forty-seven, he moved to Taos, an hour north of a Sikh center in the town of Española, to start a healing clinic. He and his wife have been living and working in New Mexico since 1998, running the yoga center and training others to teach yoga and perform massage therapies. In addition to working with children and adults, Harbhajan has also had dogs, cats, and horses as his patients.

As it had been in grade school, the memorization in acupuncture school was hard for Harbhajan. The difficulties brought back memories of school struggles. Reading books and consulting with other healers, he was diagnosed as having dyslexia and ADD. Harbhajan at last understood that his challenges in school, past and present, weren't a matter of intelligence. They had to do with the genetic makeup of his brain. "My brain processes information differently," he says matter-of-factly. "If I don't do yoga and meditation, the symptoms come up."

Happiness Is Around the Corner

Harbhajan says that he feels bad when people talk about ADD and learning differences in terms of brokenness, and he gets upset when they use words like *permanent damage* and *dysfunction*. ADD doesn't define who people are, he says, because who they are is always changing. We all develop habits to help us cope, he says. If those aren't good habits, we can change them. It's not easy, Harbhajan says, but with hard work, practice, and attention to our spirits, all people—people with or without ADD—can change. "When you give up old patterns, your life changes. Happiness is around the corner."

Harbhajan's advice to kids with ADD is that they don't have to become Sikhs to learn to handle their differences. They just need to accept and know themselves well enough not to be afraid. "Don't say, 'I'm not good enough,' or allow labels to define who you are or what you do," Harbhajan says. "Yoga has taught me to be *me*—whoever '*me*' is. 'Me' is inside my soul. That was God's will."

OMAN FRAME

Teacher

It is really important to be able to ask for help. There is no shame in that.

Date of Birth: November 12, 1971
Atlanta, Georgia

THE FIRST TIME OMAN FRAME CAUGHT A LACROSSE BALL, he knew he had found his place. "Something just clicked inside me," Oman says. "Lacrosse let me be who I am. I knew I was going to be good at it from the first day." As an African American boy with ADD growing up in the urban South in the 1970s and '80s, adults and friends expected him to listen to certain kinds of music, wear certain hairstyles and clothes, and play particular kinds of sports—basketball and football, in particular. Lacrosse, a preppy white kids' game, was *not* part of the equation.

Now a high school teacher in Atlanta, Oman looks back on his first encounter with lacrosse and realizes that it gave him a chance to stop worrying about what other people were thinking and pay closer attention to his actual feelings and needs. "I was using my entire body and thinking, too," Oman

109

remembers. "That's when I am at my best. When I can be who I am without worrying what anyone else is thinking." Like many people with ADD, Oman wondered where his true strengths were. It took some hard work, smart choices, and a lot of luck to find answers to this important question.

As a kid, Oman did poorly in school. He couldn't pay attention, and he couldn't organize his assignments and his

work. Teachers in Atlanta public schools quickly labeled Oman as "learning disabled"—a term these days he tries to avoid. True, he says, he was energetic, restless, and outspoken, but his teachers, always eager to put down young African American men, could only describe him negatively. His parents, teachers themselves, were at a loss

as to how to help. "My parents did not want to put me on medication, and they did not want to label me anything." Their strategy was to keep reassuring Oman that he learned differently, not that he couldn't learn at all.

Like a Polar Bear in the Desert

Time spent on the streets of Atlanta was as tough as time spent in the classroom. When Oman got hit in a random drive-by shooting, his parents decided they had seen enough. They both found jobs teaching in the school system on Martha's Vineyard, Massachusetts, a small island not far from Boston.

Oman was glad to move North. "No one ever understood me in Atlanta," he says. "Teachers just said, 'You're bad at this. Don't do it,' or 'You are never going to be able to read correctly,' or 'You are never going to be able to write. Look at you. You can't even write a complete sentence.'"

Once he got there, everything on Martha's Vineyard was unfamiliar and unsettling. "It was like taking a polar bear and putting it in the desert for a year," Oman says, laughing as he remembers the culture shock.

The new environment was also a blessing because he didn't have to play the role of a cool black kid anymore. "I could be who I was," he said. "I was like, 'I don't have to just listen to R&B and hip-hop and rap. I don't have to be that person anymore. I can do anything now. I can wear what I want to wear. I don't have to have my hair done a certain way.' I didn't have to be cool."

Playing Middie at Hoosac

Though some things were easier on Martha's Vineyard, other things were just the same. Even though Oman encountered less prejudice and discrimination at school, he still struggled with basic problems of organization and focus. One of his aunts taught at the Hoosac School, a private boarding school just over the Massachusetts border in rural New York. She encouraged Oman and his parents to apply, saying that Hoosac's classes of no more than eight students at a time might make a big difference for Oman. He got a full scholarship to Hoosac, which had only 120 students in grades eight through twelve, and soon his aunt's prophecy came true. With lots of structure and individualized attention, Oman's talents—and not just his shortcomings—began to emerge, and he quickly began to enjoy learning. The key for Oman was in finding a small school with teachers who were interested in helping him learn how to learn and develop his ability to think for himself.

It was at the Hoosac School that Oman first picked up a lacrosse stick. Schools in Atlanta and Martha's Vineyard hadn't offered lacrosse, but at Hoosac, lacrosse was a big deal. Oman could never have guessed when he suited up that he was about to change his life. He played "middie," the position that requires the most speed, stamina, and strategy. In lacrosse, it's up to the middies, the equivalent in soccer to the sweepers, to think of offense and defense at the same time.

"I scored a lot of goals, but I also was talented on defense," Oman remembers. "I loved the constant movement of the game. I didn't have a minute to sit back. I was always having to be aware of what was going on."

The importance of lacrosse to Oman wasn't just in athletics. Through the discipline and activity he learned in lacrosse, Oman trained himself to think more systematically, to try to see problems from more than one perspective. Most of all, Oman allowed himself to try something completely new, something that felt right to him even though it didn't fit the image others had of him. If lacrosse worked for him, then what else out there, he wondered, might be a good fit?

Falling in Love with
Learning at Hampton

That lesson took a while to stick. Although Oman had thrived at Hoosac, he fell apart in college. He made the common mistake of picking a college with a big name instead of picking a place that was a good match for his particular needs. The college he chose was huge. Oman got lost in the crowd and started failing courses. "I did horribly," Oman remembers. "I fell into the college doldrums. I didn't know my professors, and I didn't have any close friends." Even though on the outside it might've looked as if Oman didn't care about school, on the inside, he was desperate to get an education.

Yet again, an aunt stepped in to suggest a practical solution. Hampton University, a small, historically black school in Virginia with a great reputation, might be a good match for him, she said. Oman did a bit of research and agreed. Fueled by hope, Oman shut himself in his room for weeks, bringing up his grades enough to be able to meet Hampton's requirements and transfer.

As at Hoosac, at Hampton, Oman found an environment where he could thrive. Once again, small class size and individual attention made a difference. Majoring in sociology, Oman quickly got to know and like every professor in the department. And they were crazy about Oman, whose enthusiasm and great questions enlivened his classes and the department. Under these professors' careful guidance, Oman blossomed into a young intellectual, who, like the middie in lacrosse, could see the big picture and make inspiring connections. Best, with academic support and individualized attention, Oman could get back to that frame of mind where he was thinking realistically about what was right for him.

Oman remembers one teacher, in particular, Dr. Stephen Rosenthal. "He was amazing," Oman says. "He was a profound guy. He opened my eyes to the fact that I didn't have to fit the standard mold of getting a degree to make money and to buy my house and Lexus and whatever. He said, 'You can do things that will change the world.'" Professor Rosenthal urged Oman to think hard before he decided to put on a suit and tie and act like everyone else. "Ever since then," Oman says, "I have wanted to change the world."

"Do What You Want to Do"

Oman's family was thrilled with his thoughtful approach to shaping his own life. "My grandfather was alive at the time, and he said, 'Do what you want to do. Be who you are, and don't let people get in your way.'" Oman listened. He decided to try to make "Be who you are" his motto. Oman soon discovered that this was easier said than done. Watching his classmates march off to get professional degrees that would allow them to make lots of money, Oman gave in to the pressure he felt to pursue a high-status career. Though he had absolutely no interest in the law, Oman decided to go to law school and become a judge. So, he took a job working as a bailiff in a night court in Atlanta. As a bailiff, also sometimes known as a marshal or court officer, Oman was in charge of keeping order in the court, taking charge of juries when court wasn't in session, and serving legal papers.

Wanting to earn some extra money, Oman also took a job coaching during the day. What did he coach? Lacrosse, of course. He got a job at Woodward Academy, a school in the Atlanta area that had never before fielded a lacrosse team. In his first year of coaching, Oman built the lacrosse team from scratch, taking it all the way to win the state championships. Oman's night job as a bailiff bored him, while his day job as a coach filled him with positive energy and excitement. It didn't take long for Oman to know that working with kids was his true calling.

Leaving the Law

To be true to who he was, Oman had to quit his job as a bailiff. "I realized I did not want to go to law school," he said. "I said to myself, 'I want to be a teacher.'" What he loved was skateboarding, riding mountain bikes, playing lacrosse, and working with kids. "I decided it was OK not to fit the mold of a traditional black man in America," Oman says.

At about the same time, Oman began thinking deeply about what he calls "ancestral lineage traditions." He says he realized he was going through his own rite of passage by learning what career to follow. "I found different African rites of passage," Oman says. He was fascinated with ear stretching. By gradually enlarging earlobe piercings so that he could eventually insert wooden plugs the size of Lifesavers, Oman found a way to remind himself of his motto,

"Be who you are." "Most indigenous cultures have a rite of passage where you show some outward sign or adornment to demonstrate you have entered the world anew," he says. "You have gone through trials and come out a stronger person." As a teacher, he says, there's an added benefit to his earplugs: "Sure gets attention on parents' night," he says with a smile.

A Good ADD Life: Teaching and Medication

At about the same time that he switched career paths, Oman sought help from a doctor in handling ADD. He decided for the first time that he wanted to try medication. His doctor prescribed Ritalin, but he didn't like the way it made him feel. "I felt trapped," Oman says. "I definitely didn't feel like myself." Now in his thirties, Oman has given a different medication, Strattera, a try. He believes it's helping him focus better, a feeling he really likes.

It's not just medication that is helping Oman live a good life. By deciding to become a teacher, he found a way to play to his strengths. As with coaching, in teaching, Oman instinctively knows how to connect with students. "Whatever it is I am teaching, I do it *with* the kids," Oman says. "I do it with them, and I show them. I talk to them in language that's going to allow them to hear it on the basic level, and then I can elevate it to a most technical level."

With lacrosse, he says, he started by telling kids that catching a lacrosse ball was like catching an egg. "And they were like, 'Huh?' And I brought a carton of eggs out, and

I opened the carton, and I was like, 'Here! Catch!' And they were like, 'Whoa!'" After this exercise, Oman was able to say, "Okay. Now you see how you have to *give* with the egg?" The kids were nodding, he remembers, understanding in their bodies and brains precisely what their coach wanted them to do. Then Oman told them to play catch. "And they started catching eggs so they could feel it right, and they physically started to do the right move." Then Oman switched from eggs to balls. "The first thing you know, instinct kicked in," he recalls. "They were like, 'Okay, I see it.'" That's the model, he says, he likes to use whenever he teaches something new.

Without a degree in education or a teaching certificate, Oman found a job as a teaching intern at a private school outside of Boston. As always, he had a hard time with organization. Writing comments for report cards and getting papers graded were extremely tough for Oman. Teachers and administrators at the school saw more than the hard things. They witnessed Oman's gifts and believed in him deeply. "The person who believed in me most was the middle school director," Oman recalls. "He is still there now. He just said, 'You have a gift.' And I knew he was right."

Keeping on Task

Wanting to be the best teacher he could be, excited by the vote of confidence, Oman wanted to develop better strategies to cope with the hard things. Those things, he says, include maintaining focus on intense jobs, knowing when he needs to break things down and set priorities. Moving from the private school in Boston to schools in Denver and Cleveland, Oman learned to take a new approach to grading papers. "I locked myself in a room," he says. "I put myself in a situation where there wasn't any other stimulation around. I'd take a five-minute break, but then I put myself right back on task alone in that room."

Oman has great support systems these days. His best support, he says, is his wife, Naima. "She keeps me on task," he says. She loves Oman's spontaneity, creativity, and energy, but she also knows when to help him stay organized and focused. Oman also knows to look to others at work who can, as he says, give him "a nudge" and put him "back on task." People, he says, "are very accepting of this and quite willing to help me if I ask them. It is really important to be able to ask for help. There is no shame in that."

Oman is still glad he decided to stay away from law school and, instead, become a teacher. If he won the lottery, he says, he would still choose to do exactly what he's doing. "I love being a teacher because it allows me the freedom to be who I am and also to help kids who have issues similar to mine. When I reach these kids, then they can go out and change the world."

CLYDE B. ANDERSON

Chairman, Books-A-Million

Not being like everyone else, that's a good thing, not a bad thing.

Date of Birth: July 7, 1960
Montgomery, Birmingham

CLYDE ANDERSON IS TALKING ABOUT HIS BUSINESS. His eyes are wide. He is gesturing with his hands. He is describing a business deal. Clyde and his business team flew on his private jet from his home in Birmingham, Alabama, to New York. They met with twenty lawyers over the course of several days. Clyde remembers that he was thinking even faster than usual. He was in a room packed with lawyers and could listen to all their conversations at once, picking up on every detail in the room. "I was listening to one person and talking to another—it was unbelievable. In *that* type of busy environment," he says, "it was great. It just brought out everything." While in New York, Clyde never even had to go to sleep. "Oh, my goodness!" he exclaims, laughing. "I just wore 'em out!"

As the chairman of Books-A-Million, the largest discount bookstore in the Southeast, Clyde's energy has undeniably made him a public success. He took a small book business with 50 stores and expanded it into a billion-dollar business with 202 stores in eighteen states. In addition, he has managed family businesses in car dealerships, sporting goods, and fireworks. In every instance, he has made a profit. There has never been a moment, he says, when he hasn't loved what he's been doing.

Like so many people with ADD, Clyde's private life has not kept up with his public success. In a business environment—one where the stakes are high and the stimulation is even higher—he is at the height of his powers. In other environments, though, success has not come so easily. Divorced after having been married for almost twenty years, Clyde has come to see that in the same way that his ADD "wore out" his business competitors, it also "wore out" his family. Clyde has been learning more about ADD and working as hard on his relationships with his three children, his ex-wife, and his friends as he has been working on business. He has made progress, not always in a straight line, and he is working to make sure that his personal life is as successful as his professional life. Because, as Clyde knows all too well, being good at running businesses and making lots of money is not the same thing as being good at parenthood, friendship, and marriage, and being *happy*. Clyde is ready for success in these areas as well.

Family Business

Clyde always knew he would go into business. His grandfather moved from Florida to Alabama at fourteen. His great-grandfather had died unexpectedly in a barge accident, so his grandfather needed to support the family. Clyde's grandfather started selling newspapers and fireworks from a roadside stand. What started as one

newsstand grew into a big business, which his grandfather passed on to Clyde's father. Clyde's parents raised him and his three brothers on a 250-acre family estate along the Tennessee River in Florence, Alabama. The family assumed that all their sons would grow up to work in the family business. "It was sort of predestined," Clyde says, explaining that everybody in the family works in the family business. Even though Clyde grew up with plenty of money, he always knew he was expected to work. He explains how his father always had one response to everything. No matter if you're tired, sad, or sick, you go to work. "All of us worked," Clyde says. "I worked in the store from the time I was thirteen years old."

Clyde's older brothers were terrific football players who were high school all-Americans. Both of them chose to play football in college at the University of Tennessee. When it came time for Clyde to pick a college, everybody expected him to follow his brothers. But Clyde did not love football, and he was injured in his second year in high school. Just as he was about to graduate, he decided that he didn't really want to play college football. He hadn't done well in high school or given much thought to his education. Rather than following his brothers to Tennessee, Clyde went to the University of Alabama, starting out on academic probation, proving to the dean in his first semester that he could make good grades. He studied business, learning what he would need to know about finance, accounting, real estate, and law, things that would ultimately help him put together deals and make his family's business even more successful. He also met someone who believed in his academic and business abilities. One of his professors, Barry Mason, pushed Clyde to excel at business strategy, not just at making money. He remains a good friend and adviser to this day.

Breaking with Tradition

Clyde was different from his older brothers in another way. In addition to deciding not to play football and in choosing to attend the University of Alabama, Clyde also chose to join a fraternity, Kappa Alpha, a social club for men in college. For the first time, his main loyalty was not to his family. "That was probably the biggest change for me," Clyde recalls. "I had the greatest time in college." He became rush chair, the person in charge of recruiting new members—then president of the whole fraternity. Describing himself as a "social animal," Clyde says that he dated "an enormous amount" while he was in college. "I believed that it was my mission to get married in college. I thought, 'The pickings aren't getting any better than this!' I had been on this dating mission, and I worked real hard at it." He met Lisa, "the prettiest girl in school," in his first year, but it wasn't until his senior year that the two of them really discovered each other. They went out on a date; seven weeks later, Clyde asked her to marry him; and three months later, they were married.

Starting Out, Being the Boss

Clyde describes their first few years together as hard. As soon as he graduated, Clyde brought Lisa home to Florence. Florence was a small town where everybody knew Clyde's family, and it wasn't easy for Lisa, an outsider, to find her place. She had always worked, and even though Clyde's family had plenty of money, she continued to work. Clyde plunged back into the family business with the goal of moving parts of the business from Florence to Montgomery, a bigger town with what Clyde believed would be greater opportunities.

Four years after they had married, Clyde and Lisa had their first child—Ali, a daughter—and made good on Clyde's promise to take his businesses to Montgomery. Within several years, Clyde and Lisa had two more children, Olivia and Christian, and Lisa continued to work. Clyde would get up early, leaving the house before 7:00 in the morning, and often he would not be back home until 7:30 or 8:00 at night. The business was growing by leaps and bounds. Clyde traveled from store to store and state to state several days a week. He regularly talked on the phone to all of his store managers, at times having eight or ten phone lines going at once. He checked e-mails, held board meetings, and worked hard to be the boss. Busy all the time, constantly making decisions, Clyde continued to set high goals for himself and his companies.

Clyde says he met most of these goals, because he knew, on his own, how to manage the symptoms he now understands come from ADD. He hired a bright and organized personal secretary to keep track of details. He only reads important documents when he travels on his personal airplane. The sound of the engine and the motion help keep him still and focused. He discovered that the allergy medication his doctor prescribed had similar effects to Ritalin, which helped him concentrate. Since he controlled his business meetings, he could cut things short when he lost interest. All of these things, he now knows, helped him manage his ADD at work.

Trouble at Home:
Breaking Things to Fix Them

Clyde had trouble at home, where the level of stimulation wasn't as high as it was at work. He needed to listen to his wife, sharing power in his marriage, but this was hard for Clyde. He couldn't relax or hang out with his kids because he always wanted to be on the go. He liked being "the boss," finishing other people's sentences before they could say what they were thinking. He realized that he needed to be stimulated all the time, and if he was bored, he'd "break things"— pick fights, make people mad at him—just so he'd have a chance to "fix things." He liked the excitement of getting a chance to heal the hurts, to send flowers and start over again. Thinking back, he realizes that worked for only so long.

When Clyde read about ADD, he suspected that he had it. He consulted with a psychiatrist, who agreed with Clyde. When drug companies stopped making the allergy medicine Clyde had been taking for years, Clyde asked his doctor if he could try some of the typical medications people take for ADD. Some of them have made him feel funny, but others are working better. He's continuing to try different medications, knowing that it may take a while before he's settled on the right combination for him.

The Best Strategy of All

"The best thing that's happened is finally admitting that I have ADD," Clyde says. He understands now what it takes to make a relationship work. He is learning that he needs to find excitement without "breaking things." He has also cut back at work, knowing that if he has to have excitement in his life, he wants to find it in his children. These days, instead of getting to work before the sun is up, Clyde first drives his children to school. He's also coaching soccer and trying to find ways to hang out with them more. His gifts from ADD are great—"I can do a deal like nobody's business," he says—but so are his weaknesses.

Clyde has a better sense of his strengths and weaknesses now, and he wants to make sure that he has a chance to work as hard on them as he has on his business.

Clyde wants kids to know that he's aware how hard it is to be different. He also wants them to know that being different can also be great. "Not being like everyone else," he says, "that's a good thing, not a bad thing." His advice is that kids with ADD try to accept what is hard and figure out how they work best. "If you find you read better with the TV on, and everybody tells you you're not supposed to, ignore them and do what's right for you." That may take awhile, Clyde says, "but stick with it! It's worth it in the end!"

JON BONNELL

Chef

I wasn't dumb or lazy.
I just couldn't focus.

Date of Birth: November 15, 1970
Fort Worth, Texas

JON BONNELL THOUGHT HE HAD EVERYTHING FIGURED OUT.
He'd graduated from Vanderbilt University in Tennessee with
a degree to teach middle school science. And he was doing
what he supposedly wanted to do. He'd moved home to Texas
and was teaching science at the Winston School, a place spe-
cializing in teaching kids with learning differences. He loved
the kids. They loved him. Really. But at 3:00, when the
school day ended, Jon was at his wits' end. He'd already gotten his lesson plans together. He'd finished his grading. He'd
look around and scratch his head. "I really liked it. I did," he
says. "But I was bored. I'd watch TV, go to sleep. I was going
nuts." Summers were worse, he says. "I was twenty-five years
old, and it was just me and the dog. I said to myself, 'Now's
the time to get after it.'"

I Wanted to Be the Guy
Who Could Do All of It!

Jon already knew he had ADD, and he knew that to be happy, he needed to do something, as he says, with "high intensity" and very little downtime. He knows it sounds a little hard to believe, but he—the big, strapping football player and enthusiastic crossbow hunter—had always loved to watch cooking shows on TV. "I'd even make the dishes," he says. "In college, I was the only one who knew how to cook." What would it be like, he wondered, to train to be a chef and run his own restaurant? He bought a guide to culinary schools that suggested getting a restaurant job to make sure cooking professionally was the right move. Jon took the advice and asked for a leave of absence from school to work in a restaurant kitchen helping to get plates out to diners. After three and a half months, Jon was sure: "This was my world!"

Being in a professional kitchen reminded John of a big game of Tetris or a three-ring circus. "There were five guys on the line on one side of the kitchen, five guys on the other side. Everything was happening at the same time, all at once. We fed three hundred people a night, and it didn't seem like time passed. I just fell in love with it." Jon said he felt great standing up, moving around, flying back and forth across the kitchen. The expediter—the person who makes sure the kitchen runs effectively and smoothly—would check the plates to make sure the orders were correct, arranging food so that it looked just right. "It was like he was conducting a symphony," Jon says, awe in his voice. "I wanted to be the guy who could do *all* of it."

The next step, Jon says, was to find the right school. Without telling anyone, including his family, what he was thinking about doing, Jon took a look at various schools. The one he liked most was the New England Culinary Institute. "It was the dream school for me. There was *no* classwork. No bookwork. It was *all* hands-on. Everything was pass/fail. You repeated skills until you were proficient. It was the perfect environment for *me*."

Underachieving, Big-Time

Jon knew a lot about himself as a learner. School had never come easily, which was especially hard because his older brother and sister had been academic stars. His teachers noted early on that he seemed to talk a lot in class, didn't stay organized, and rarely turned in his homework on time, if at all. Testing showed John's parents that he was bright, had ADD, and was dysgraphic. "That basically means I had terrible handwriting," Jon says. His parents eventually bought him

a computer, and Jon learned to touch-type. But they didn't believe in the ADD diagnosis and didn't tell him about it. "Hey, it was the 1970s," Jon says forgivingly. "People in Fort Worth were just beginning to diagnose ADD." Jon says the story at school was always the same: he did the bare minimum, the least he could just to get by.

Jon knew, deep inside, that it wasn't in his nature to be the lazy guy with C– grades. By the time he hit high school, he was frustrated with his lackluster performance. He asked his parents to send him to boarding school in Massachusetts so that he'd have a better shot at going to college. Though they were surprised, Jon's parents helped him find a good place where he worked hard and pulled up his grades. He went on to Vanderbilt from boarding school.

Once in college, without the rigid structure of boarding school, Jon reverted to his old ways. "It was just the same thing," he says. "I did the least amount of work to get by." He joined a fraternity—a social club—and made good friends. He first chose "human development" as his major, which, he says, was what most of the football team majored in, to be able to teach gym. At the end of his second year, Jon had a change of heart. "I was getting serious, thinking more about careers." He decided he was most interested in education, wanting to teach science in middle school because "this is where kids get lost."

Where Do I Go to Get Some Testing Done?

About halfway through his first semester as an education major, in the fall of 1992, Jon read a chapter about ADD in one of his education textbooks. He remembers saying out loud, "*This* is the story of my life! This describes exactly *me!*" Without thinking twice, Jon set out to have himself tested. "I went from department to department, asking the same question over and over again: 'Where do I go to get some testing done?'" After several weeks, he managed to get referred to a psychologist in town. "I was living off campus with some guys. I didn't tell anyone. I didn't even call home." The psychologist put Jon through six hours of testing and then asked him to gather as many of his old school reports as possible.

At that point, he telephoned his mom and told her what he was doing. "She was totally willing to help me," he says. "And of course, she had it all—every teacher's description of me, all the written report cards." The reports said exactly the same thing, Jon says. "I was this nice, bright, pleasant, disorganized, distracted person." The psychologist confirmed the diagnosis that Jon had never known about. "He said it was clear-cut. I had ADD."

I Wasn't Dumb or Lazy

The next step was a little harder. He had the information and the diagnosis. What was he going to do with it? He read as much as he could about ADD and then decided he wanted to try medication. A doctor wrote him a prescription for ten milligrams of short-acting Ritalin to take three times a day. At the drugstore, the pharmacist looked at Jon oddly. "'This is for *you?*' he asked. Ten, fifteen years ago," Jon says, "almost nobody was thinking about *adults* with ADD." They figured ADD was a problem for kids, who they thought generally outgrew the symptoms. Not so, doctors say these days. The pharmacist went to a safe to get the Ritalin. Jon felt like he was about to take something more dangerous than addictive painkillers. After all he'd read, after all the testing and talking with doctors, Jon decided he would give it a try.

"I went back to my apartment and asked my roommates for the biggest, fattest, dullest, political science textbook they could find," Jon says. He took the Ritalin and opened the book. Ordinarily, he says, he'd never have gotten through the first page. "I'd always either doze off or be thinking about a million things, hunting trips, answering the phone, whatever." This time, though, Jon says, he just sat there and read straight through for an hour. Then he read the study guide questions, and he could answer every single one of them correctly. He was, he says, in a state of complete and total shock. He remembers thinking, "This is *great*! I have *finally* figured out what I have got!"

The figuring out part was the most important part, Jon says. "Being able to take Ritalin was the bonus." By the end of the semester, Jon's grade-point average had shot up. Instead of getting Cs and C–s, his last two years of college, Jon consistently earned marks ranging from B+ to A. He threw himself into his studies and, for the first time in his life, didn't procrastinate or try to get by doing the least possible amount of work. "I *wasn't* dumb or lazy," he says. "I just couldn't focus."

Acing Culinary School

Understanding exactly how his brain worked, Jon knew when he enrolled in culinary school what he would need to do to be successful. He had found something he loved, something with the perfect amount of stimulation, and with Ritalin, he knew how to stay focused and to work effectively. "I decided I was going to graduate at the top of the class," he says matter-of-factly. "And I did." It didn't matter to Jon if he was assigned to work a 5:00 a.m. breakfast shift or was closing out at 11:00 at night. When he worked "chef's table" and had to make a completely new menu on his own every day, Jon was in heaven. "To me, it was simple," he says. "I got to be creative. I worked great under pressure. And I developed a lot of confidence."

To earn his degree, Jon completed two internships in restaurants. The first was in a fast-paced, fancy restaurant in the French Quarter in New Orleans. He trained in hot appetizers, at the grill, as a sauté chef, and then in food preparation. The second was back home, in Forth Worth, at a forty-seat restaurant downtown. "If it was hot," Jon says, "I made it."

One of Jon's favorite assignments in culinary school was to design a concept for a restaurant. "I told them, 'Hey, I've got a place in mind already.'" Jon wanted to open a relatively small, fine restaurant featuring fresh foods native to Texas. His vision was to partner with farmers who could provide him with the freshest fruits and vegetables in season—things like heirloom tomatoes and Texas's famous Parker County peaches—and with ranchers who could breed deer and quail, animals plentiful around Fort Worth. From this assignment, Jon put together his vision of what he wanted to do after he graduated in 1998.

Bonnell's Fine Texas Cuisine

With the help of family and friends, Jon opened his own restaurant, Bonnell's Fine Texas Cuisine, in Fort Worth. It took him a few years to raise the money and find the property. In the meantime, he cooked in friends' restaurants, catered parties, and worked as a personal chef, fixing meals for private clients. He bought an old bank building and turned it into his restaurant, which he opened October 12, 2001. The bank vault now serves as his wine cellar.

A typical workday for Jon begins at about 9:30 a.m., when he arrives at the restaurant. He spends about an hour on the phone and computer. By 10:30, Jon sets the day's specials and finishes paperwork. He meets with staff at 10:45, and the restaurant begins serving lunch at 11:00. Generally, Jon's in the kitchen, overseeing everything. Menus include entrees such as pecan-crusted Texas redfish, shrimp-and-scallop enchiladas with crawfish beignets, and desserts including caramel-pecan cheesecake and fresh berry empanadas with huckleberry cream. He likes working with the staff, he says, because he "gets to be a teacher again." Lunch ends between 1:30 and 2:00.

Jon then takes a break from the kitchen for a few hours. On Tuesdays, Jon checks wine and liquor inventories and places orders, and on Wednesdays, he has a meeting to talk with restaurant decision makers. Jon also draws up proposals to cater weddings, creates new recipes and menus, runs to the bank and post office, or picks up stray supplies such as wood chips for smoking meats. He tries to make sure, no matter what, that he has time to see his wife, Melinda, a former book publisher, who generally works at the restaurant in the evenings. He's always back at the restaurant by 5:00 or 5:30 p.m. to gear up for dinner.

In the late afternoons, Jon often tends bar, but by dinnertime, he works as the expediter, making sure everything runs smoothly in the kitchen. He usually visits tables in the dining room, and he loves to get a chance to recommend wines to accompany various items on the menu. Closing time is at about 11:00 each night. After that, Jon heads home to sleep before another busy day. The restaurant is closed on Sundays and Mondays, Jon says, so that he, his wife, and his staff don't get burned out. In his spare time, Jon hunts, fishes, and takes photographs of wildlife.

A Recipe for Success: Lists and Notes

Even with this schedule, Jon still has a hard time staying organized. "I'll go on a hunting trip without a bow," he says. "One hour down the road, I'll realize I left the bow sitting in the middle of the driveway. I'll take off golfing without the clubs. I mean, I'll have the golf shoes *on*, and the clubs will still be sitting in the house. I'll leave drinks on the top of the car, take off, and spill everything. You know, I'll go to the dry cleaner, take half the stuff that needs cleaning, and leave the rest on the floor—or I'll lose the claim check." Melinda "can be frustrated about ADD stuff," Jon says. "It gets old pretty quick."

People may wonder, Jon says, how an impulsive, distracted, restless person with ADD can keep track of all the details involved in running a restaurant. Jon says that when you know the trouble spots, you cope. Jon's two best strategies? Lists and notes, he says. "If I make a list, I can do it." For instance, say he is catering a function, and he needs fifty or hundred different ingredients. "I make a list of everything we have to take. I make sure it's all in the car. If I just throw it in and go, I'm guaranteed to fail." Jon keeps a pen in his shirt pocket and writes himself notes all day, telling himself when he needs to have payroll ready, when he needs to get change from the bank, whom he needs to phone, what should go on various menus. The notes go in his top shirt pocket, and he continually checks them throughout the day. At night, the notes sit next to his keys, which go next to his cell phone, which rests next to his wallet. In his wallet, he's always got his hunting license, driver's license, checks—the things, he says, he always needs. Ritalin still comes in handy, Jon says, although he only takes it once or twice a week when he has to pay bills for three hours straight or clean out the garage. If he has to focus on something he really hates doing, Jon takes his medicine and finishes his tasks promptly, without a lot of fuss.

With hard work and insight, Jon has come up with a recipe for success. His restaurant is doing well, his marriage is strong, and he's still having fun. The culinary world has noticed. He's been invited twice to cook at the James Beard House in Greenwich Village, New York, a center for cutting-edge cuisine. Jon also regularly teaches cooking classes and serves as guest host on television cooking shows he used to love to watch. It's all going great, Jon says, because he hasn't used ADD as an excuse to do nothing. "It's not a disability," he says. "It's a difference."

LINDA PINNEY

Entrepreneur, Chief Business Officer, Asteres

*I really couldn't help it.
I didn't want to cause
so much trouble.*

Date of Birth: March 15, 1962
Del Mar, California

IN SECOND GRADE, LINDA PINNEY FELT REALLY BAD for the kids in her class who were having a hard time with subtraction. She raised her hand, as she so often did, and her teacher ignored her—as *she* so often did. Linda kept raising her hand. And her teacher kept ignoring her. Student and teacher were, yet again, locked in a stalemate.

"The hundredth time my hand was up, I stood up in my chair," Linda says. "'Do you know,' I told her, 'that there is a *much simpler way* to do this? That this is *all wrong?*'" As usual, Linda's teacher got really mad. "'Well,' my teacher said, 'would *you* like to come up and teach the class and show us?'" Linda didn't hear the sarcasm in her teacher's voice and eagerly leaped to the chalkboard. After she showed the kids her special method of subtraction, the angry teacher exploded and sent Linda to the principal's office.

"I was devastated," Linda remembers, still outraged almost forty years later. "I felt crushed." Her intentions had been so good. All she'd wanted to do, she says, was to show everybody a simpler, better way to do something routine. What a shame that she was punished for doing the very thing she does best.

Now a successful entrepreneur, Linda has spent her adult life creating products in health care that show people how to do simple things better. She is the founder and chief business officer of Asteres, a company in California that makes ATM-style machines to dispense prescription drugs. With a team of engineers, Linda figured out a safe way to save people time at the drugstore so they wouldn't have to wait in line to pick up their prescription refills.

Her Own Special Homeroom

As an adult with ADD, Linda can arrange her life so that she can stand on chairs and shout out answers to her heart's content. As a kid with ADD, though, Linda spent much of her time in what she af-fectionately calls her "own special homeroom"—the principal's office, which she "visited" at least three times a week. Only in adulthood, with a lot of help, has Linda been able to craft a life that allows her to translate her good intentions into actions that others welcome.

Even though Linda knew her parents adored her, she also knew that she was a handful. When Linda recently visited her parents, they showed her videos they'd taken of her as a child growing up. "I was just running in circles," Linda says. Her mom told her that she was never still, except when she was sleeping—which also was rare. "I think my mom would just stare at me and say, 'Oh, my God! What is it? Where did it come from?'" Linda says, laughing. "I was the first child and the *only* child. I don't think that was planned until *after* I arrived."

Harnessing Boundless Energy

Once Linda was old enough to play sports, her parents signed her up for anything and everything to help harness their daughter's boundless energy. "I wasn't a group sports person," she says. "I tried to play soccer, but I forgot there was anyone else on the field but me. Let's just say I was *not* great at passing." With practice, Linda became a competitive swimmer and tennis player. "No doubles," she says forcefully. Regular, vigorous exercise was "a big help" as she tried to get through her days at school.

The other things that helped were chores. At home and at school, adults found things for Linda to do. Linda took care of the many family pets, made her bed, cleaned her room, took dishes to the kitchen sink, folded towels, sorted socks, and helped put things away. By the time she was eight, Linda had learned to mow and edge the lawn, rake and bag leaves, and skim the swimming pool. Linda's mom bought extra workbooks, which Linda could do at home or school. Secretaries in the principal's office had her make copies, fill up the ink on the mimeograph machine, and run notes to classrooms.

Despite her parents' and teachers' efforts, Linda continued to get in trouble. That didn't mean Linda hated school. "I *loved* going to school!" Linda says. "I did like to learn. I loved getting to be with people. I was very, very good at math and science." Smart as a whip, Linda was just so disruptive and impulsive that teachers often noticed the bad things instead of the good. A blurter, she complained about things she found repetitious and boring.

Pink Slips

By junior high, when she had to change classrooms every period, Linda was never where she was supposed to be. "All of a sudden, I'd be late. Not *very* late—maybe five minutes, just enough to be irritating. Class would have started, everybody would be sitting down, and I'd just be coming in." Linda would try to slip in unnoticed, but that strategy rarely worked. A great talker, Linda would then try to negotiate her way out of trouble. That didn't work very well either.

Over the years, Linda collected more pink slips than any other student in the history of her high school. She says the worst part was that she really and truly wasn't trying to be a problem. Linda was oblivious to the effects her actions had on others. She could never figure out, for instance, how she managed to reduce teachers to tears. Her parents and teachers "just didn't understand how I could be so unaware," Linda says, "that I really couldn't help it. I didn't want to cause so much trouble."

No one ever said Linda had ADD, but they did suggest over and over that her parents put her on Ritalin. Linda's dad rejected that plan. "He'd be like, 'She doesn't have any problems. She's just a little active.'" At the same time, she says, her dad was embarrassed and exasperated by her behavior. In business and sales, he often traveled during the week, coming home on weekends to find that, yet again, Linda was in trouble for wreaking havoc at school.

Linda doesn't blame her parents for not following through on a formal diagnosis of ADD or putting her on medication. "They always kept my spirit high," she says. "They disciplined me, set limits, made me go to class, but they never put me down. They never ever stopped telling me how great I was, how good I would be, how I would really be something someday."

The first time Linda had an inkling that she was more than just a troublemaker came when she was graduating from high school. There was an awards ceremony at which the school handed out three prizes: one to the person with the best grades, one to the person who had performed the greatest acts of service, and one to the person with the greatest leadership potential. A friend was going to be given the award for highest grades. Linda wanted to be there to cheer her on. Unshowered, Linda snuck into the back of the gym and scrunched herself into a corner. When it came time for the leadership award, the principal called out Linda's name. She was literally stunned beyond belief. "I mean, *I* was the kid the French teacher dragged to the principal by the *ear* for back-talking," Linda says. "I figured they couldn't wait to get rid of me." As she walked to the front of the gym she saw that the secretaries made streamers of all her pink slips by taping them together, then the vice principal stood on a chair and dropped a row of them from each hand that cascaded across the floor. Able to see her strengths as well as her failings, the school let Linda know that they applauded the best in her.

College and Graduate School: Do Whatever You Want

In college, Linda enjoyed the freedom to do what she liked. Deciding on genetics, or the study of DNA, for her major, Linda went to the University of California at Davis. Always on the go, Linda played sports, started an on-campus cable company, and sought out others to have fun. She didn't go to class very often, she says, but nobody seemed to mind so long as she kept up her grades. Still plagued by disorganization, Linda would sometimes sit in on the wrong class or show up at the wrong place to take exams. Linda tended to put off work until the last minute, stay up all night, and hand in her work. "I never took drugs or drank," she says, "but I did pound down the coffee."

During this time of freedom and exploration Linda realized that she was gay. She fell in love her sophomore year. Living in an apartment complex off campus, she met Cathy, a psychology major. That was more than twenty years ago. The two have been a couple ever since.

Torn between medical school and business school after college, Linda took entrance tests for a wide variety of graduate and professional schools—the GRE, the GMAT, the MCAT—and scored high on all of them. In the end, she decided to attend the University of Southern California in Los Angeles because the school said "the magic words, 'Do whatever you want.'" Thrilled, Linda spent two years getting two master's degrees, one in business and another in health care administration.

Working Best in the Face of NO

The more control Linda had over her life and her work, the better things kept getting. Linda worked for a health care system for a while, but she got restless. She jumped at the chance to be an entrepreneur, a person, Linda says, "who works best in the face of NO." Linda likes to take ideas and turn them into actual products, "going from nothing to something." Her parents weren't thrilled. "Telling your parents you want to be an entrepreneur," Linda says, "is sort of like telling your parents you're going to be an artist. It just seems too seat-of-the-pants, too free-flying." As Linda has experienced success, her parents have stopped worrying. This is always easier, she says, when parents know their kids are safe and happy.

Linda's had a chance to work on a wide variety of products. One of the first was a portable call button for elderly people in nursing homes. Linda developed drug-dispensing stations for hospitals. Then she found a way to help patients to have DNA testing done more efficiently and cheaply. When that company "went public," allowing anyone to invest, Linda made millions of dollars. Linda felt the freedom to continue thinking up better ways to do things, the grown-up version of showing her fellow second graders how to subtract.

Linda's workday hasn't ever really been a "day," she says. She generally sleeps until 9:00 or 9:30 in the morning, when her two golden retrievers and rabbit wake her. She makes telephone calls, checks e-mails, and drinks lots and lots of coffee. Her assistant generally calls her by late morning— often to tell her that she's late for something. "I try to get to the office by 11:30 or 12:00," she says. She goes out for lunch with a friend or business contact, and then focuses on customers, contracts, and deals. She spends the bulk of her day with people in her company, looking for solutions to problems and obstacles they've identified. Near the end of the day, she takes her dogs out for a run, and then she has dinner. After that, Linda says, she really gets to work. Between 7:00 or 8:00 at night and 2:00 or 3:00 in the morning, Linda is at her most productive.

Making Some Big Changes

Linda bubbled along until two bad things happened a few years ago. Linda left a company she founded because she didn't agree with the direction the business was heading. Unhappy without work, Linda was miserable at home. After nearly twenty years together, Cathy decided she couldn't live with Linda unless Linda made some big changes.

Linda sought help from a therapist who finally confronted

her about having ADD. "He said, 'So, tell me, what do you do for your ADD.' And I said, 'What? Why do you say that?' He said, 'Well, you *do* have ADD.' And I said, 'No.' And he said, 'Let me just state this for you. You *have* ADD.'" Linda was floored. She says that even though there had been plenty of "wreckage points along the way" in their relationship, neither she nor Cathy—a psychologist—had ever thought about addressing Linda's behaviors in terms of ADD. The counselor gave Linda a book to read. "I was actually depressed enough to sit still and read it," she says. "I looked up and said, 'Oh, my God! That's *me!*'"

Linda found a psychiatrist to prescribe medication. The doctor she liked best specializes in children. She seemed to know more about ADD than anyone else and was most familiar with medications. Linda now takes Adderall in the day and Strattera at night, to help her sleep.

Wanting to Be Good

While Linda says she has benefited tremendously from medications, and while she can see how helpful both the formal diagnosis and the meds would have been in her childhood, there is still a part of her that struggles with what she's come to know. "I spent forty years running along at a certain pace, with a certain level of awareness—or lack of awareness—and then that changed," she says. Slowed down by medication, Linda actually notices and feels a lot more. Not all of what she notices feels good, though. Being aware of how much she took her relationship with Cathy for granted is terribly painful. Without the awareness and pain, though, Linda doesn't think she'd have been able to change her behavior enough to get back together with Cathy, which means more to her than anything in the world. It's also helped her start her new company.

Linda knows, on some level, that what was true for her at seven is true for her in her forties. She didn't intentionally set about inflicting pain on anyone—not on her second-grade teacher, not on Cathy. She *wanted* to be good. Without a diagnosis of ADD and medications, though, she truly was not capable of reining in her impulsivity and considering other people's feelings. Sometimes, she feels less creative and, in her words, less "freewheeling" on medications, but the trade-off for her is that she's so much better able to control her impulsivity and enjoy other people.

Linda knows how hard it is to work on impulsive behavior and speech. Her advice to kids is that even though much of what they have to say is right, they have to think about *when* they say it. "There's probably a really good place for it, and sometimes it might even be when you blurt it out," she says. "But there're times when it might *not* be a good time. The *timing* is sometimes as important as the thing you want to say or do."

CLARENCE PAGE

Journalist, Chicago Tribune

Having ADD is like having fifty TV sets going in my head at once. Ritalin works by turning off forty-nine of them.

Date of Birth: June 2, 1947
Washington, DC

CLARENCE PAGE CAN'T DISCUSS ADD WITHOUT TALKING about his son, Grady. Like so many adults confronting ADD later in life, Clarence, a Pulitzer Prize–winning journalist, found himself in a doctor's office getting tested because of his child's diagnosis. Knowing that ADD is almost always inherited from family members (it's more inheritable than height), Clarence and his wife, Lisa, wondered who else in the family might have ADD. "We talked about this from the very beginning. We said, 'Mom and Dad may have ADD, too,'" Clarence says. "And Lisa would say, 'Yeah, mainly *Dad!*'"

A bright, verbal, winning boy, Grady had had a hard time in grade school. Clarence and Lisa were confused. "He was *so* articulate. He *sounded* so bright. He had such a *big* vocabulary," Clarence says, "and he was so much like *us.*" The only way Clarence could account for his son's difficulties was to blame his behavior. When teachers suggested Grady had a learning difference, Clarence and Lisa were stunned. "I mean, how could he *possibly* have had a learning disability?" Despite their misgivings, Clarence and Lisa had Grady tested and learned that he had ADD. And then, he says, it dawned on his wife and on him that if Grady could have ADD . . . well, so could Clarence.

Fathers of Sons with ADD

They followed their doctor's advice, putting Grady on medication and moving him to the Lab School, a special, private school dedicated to teaching kids with learning differences. Two years later, Lisa prodded Clarence to attend a talk at the school. "It was called something like 'Fathers of Sons with ADD,'" Clarence recalls. Upon hearing the doctor's lecture, Clarence noted that he did exhibit most of the signs of ADD. He was maddeningly disorganized. He needed lots of deadlines to help him hand in work, most of it at the last minute. Able to manage short bursts of concentration, Clarence couldn't sustain his attention long enough to finish complicated, drawn-out projects. In his office, he usually has a computer, several TV shows, and the radio going at once, constantly bouncing from thing to thing to keep from getting bored. "I like it like that," he says, "but it drives my wife crazy."

After the presentation at the school, Clarence introduced himself to the doctor, who agreed to evaluate him in his office. "The testing was pretty quick," Clarence recalls. "It had a lot to do with focus and attention." Sure enough, the doctor told Clarence that his hunch had been right. The doctor told Clarence that he had ADD.

You might wonder why someone as successful and accomplished as Clarence would care about finding out he had ADD. After all, Clarence, a nationally syndicated newspaper columnist for the *Chicago Tribune*, had already experienced an extraordinary amount of public success. He had won not *one* but *two* Pulitzer Prizes for his journalism, the top award for his field. In 1996, he'd published a terrific book, *Showing My Color: Impolite Essays on Race and Identity*. Clarence was regularly asked to appear on television talk shows such as *The NewsHour with Jim Lehrer* and *The MacLaughlin Group*. What difference could it possibly have made to Clarence whether he knew he had ADD?

The Four Benefits of Knowing

Believe it or not, Clarence says, knowing that he has ADD has helped in four important ways.

First and foremost, he says, it's helped him understand his son better. "When Grady was diagnosed, I was in big denial about it. I thought, 'Well, they're either overdiagnosing him, or he's not trying hard enough, or he just needs to work harder and concentrate harder'—all the things my father told me. Now I really understand this condition," Clarence says. "Before I understood it from the inside out, I was more demanding of Grady. I don't get overupset any more about the kinds of mistakes he makes." Clarence is able to show Grady that he makes mistakes too. He can also share coping and compensating strategies. He gives Grady advice ("Which he never listens to," Clarence adds), suggesting that he do the hardest tasks first. "Get them out of the way." And if you can't figure out how to do the hard stuff? "If it seems to stop you for now," he says, "move on. Break it into small tasks."

Which leads Clarence to the second benefit he's gotten from his diagnosis. Knowing he has ADD, Clarence says, has provided practical benefits. Before he knew he had ADD, Clarence smoked cigarettes and drank a lot of coffee, which tended to calm him down and keep his mind from wandering. Knowing that he has ADD, he can take medications to stay more focused while cutting out the unhealthy stuff— especially the cigarettes. "Having ADD," he says, "is like having fifty TV sets going in my head at once. Ritalin works," he explains, "by turning off forty-nine of them."

Knowing more about his brain and having medications that help him tune out distractions, Clarence says he's more efficient. Rather than starting in on five things at once— balancing his checkbook, researching his columns, writing, returning telephone calls, sending e-mails—and finishing none of them until the last minute, now Clarence knows to "take on one task at a time." He tries to follow his own advice, and at the bare minimum, he says, he's more organized— "although I'm not as organized as I could be. That's helpful at home and professionally."

Third, he says, his diagnosis has helped with "human relationships." The whole world looks different, he says, when you reevaluate what "normal" is. Maybe he's a little more forgiving, and he has more patience for other people's differences. "It's a lot easier to judge," Clarence says, "than it is to understand." He makes a comparison between prejudices against people of color and people with learning differences. "I grew up as a black kid in America in the fifties and sixties. People wanted to put me in a box, expecting me to be a certain way," Clarence says. "I was always fighting against that. I see the same things happening to kids with ADD." People expect them to act and learn a certain way, but they don't. They have to fight to figure out who they are and what they need. "Every child learns differently," Clarence says. "I've gone through my own personal evolution in understanding how that works."

Fourth and last, Clarence says, he is better able to understand himself: "I am working to accept my limitations and my strengths." That's complicated, because Clarence is ambitious and still feels he has lots to accomplish. It starts, though, with looking back at his childhood and cutting himself a little slack.

Everything Looked Like an Ashtray

Clarence wishes he'd known he had ADD when he was a kid growing up in Middletown, Ohio. Maybe he'd have been a little easier on himself. Clarence wanted to be like all the other boys. Back then, he says, most of the boys wanted to be engineers. Never mind that he was bored stiff by higher math and science. Everyone was talking about the space race and the

Soviet Union's Sputnik, the first human-made satellite to orbit the earth. Clarence thought he should be an engineer, too. Boys took wood shop and metal shop. Everything Clarence made, he says, looked like an ashtray. He remembers his metal-shop teacher telling him, in eighth grade, "We're not very good with our hands, are we, Page?" His teacher's comment stung.

For career day in high school, Clarence, of course, tried to sign up for the engineering section. Some part of him was happy when he found out it was full. There were plenty of spots in the journalism section, and one of his teachers gave him a nudge to attend. The only boy in the room, Clarence was immediately hooked. Thinking about current events, Clarence got excited—far more excited than he'd ever gotten about Sputnik. President John F. Kennedy had been assassinated, the Beatles were appearing on the *Ed Sullivan Show* on TV, and college students were protesting racial segregation in the South. "I wanted to be a part of it."

Writing for Newspapers: The Perfect Match

From then on, journalism—writing for daily newspapers—became Clarence's thing. He started writing for his high school newspaper, and then, after he graduated from high school, he earned a college degree in journalism from Ohio University in 1969. Working his way up as a reporter from small papers to the *Chicago Tribune*, Clarence eventually became a columnist and an editorial board member. These days, he writes two short columns a week about anything that interests him, and as a member of the paper's editorial board, he writes two short, unsigned pieces a week about something the paper's senior editors think needs discussing.

Looking back on his career choice, knowing now that he has ADD, Clarence says journalism was a "perfect" match for him. "The writing is short," he says. "There's always a deadline." That makes it a lot easier to stay on track. In fact, Clarence says, he suspects newsrooms in the old days were filled with people with ADD. He calls it "newsroom syndrome." "Newsmen," he says, "were always a bunch of hard drinkers and hard smokers. They were wonderful characters. There was such high adventure to it all." Clarence figures they thrived on the noisy, raucous newsroom and that they could use their high energy levels to meet the fast-and-furious pace of daily deadlines. They probably drank and smoked so much to deal with symptoms of ADD. "Everything's changed so much," he says. "Reporters are business professionals now. They're really elegant specialists. They come in with master's degrees in economics and art history now. They've been to law school. They're very bright, but there sure is a lot less noise." Nowadays, Clarence says, the old-timers think newsrooms are like "insurance companies" because they are so orderly and quiet.

Though Clarence did well in school—"It was easier back then," he says—there were so many things he couldn't and still can't do. "Books are hard for me," he says. Clarence hasn't been able to focus long enough, he says, to read classics—complicated, long novels such as Leo Tolstoy's *Anna Karenina* or Herman Melville's *Moby Dick*. "My son asked me if I'd read my own book," Clarence says, "and the answer was, 'Cover to cover? No.'" Obviously a very bright person, Clarence could not find a single reason other than lack of intelligence for what he viewed as his failures. "I felt so ashamed and embarrassed and inadequate," Clarence says. "Had I been more aware," he says, "I'd either have forgiven myself or figured out different strategies."

A Novel Approach

Clarence says that if he'd had a better sense of how his brain worked, he'd have tried some different things. He always wanted to go to law school, not necessarily to be a lawyer, but at the very least to have a better appreciation for America's legal system. Since he didn't do well on standardized tests, he figured he wasn't smart enough to get into law school. Clarence says he believes he could go to law school now, if he wanted, but that he thinks he's got too many other things going on in his life.

Clarence wishes more kids heard the message that if they understand how their minds work and how they learn, they really can grow up to be whatever they want: "It can't be said enough." He thinks a lot about people he's met who've spent time in jail. As kids, he says, none of them ever said they wanted to get in trouble. "*Nobody* says they *want* to be a burgler or a con man. If you ask kids, they'll tell you they want to be a doctor, a lawyer, a computer programmer, an electrician, a teacher, or a car mechanic. Things go wrong when we tell them, 'No, you can't do it. You're worthless.'"

Clarence takes this stuff seriously, for other kids and for Grady, too. He knows it would be all too easy for some teacher somewhere these days to look at a boy like Grady and decide that because he has ADD, he can't succeed. Clarence is glad he knows enough about ADD to allow himself and his son to reach for the stars. He's delighted that Grady's taken an interest in journalism, writing pieces in his school newspaper about Dungeons and Dragons and the fighting in Afghanistan. As for Clarence, he's aiming high, too. He's hard at work writing his first novel.

Resources

For more information about and support for ADD, consider contacting the following organizations:

Attention Deficit Disorder Association (ADDA)
P.O. Box 543, Pottstown, PA 19464
484-945-2101
www.add.org
Primarily advocates and provides support and information for adults with ADD.

Attention Deficit Disorder Resources
223 Tacoma Avenue S #100, Tacoma, WA 98402
253-759-5085
www.addresources.org
Support and education for those with ADD.

Children and Adults with Attention Deficit Disorder (CHADD)
8181 Professional Place, Ste. 150, Landover, MD 20785
301-306-7070
www.chadd.org
Large national organization with local chapters, which promotes research into ADD and informs, advocates, and educates.

National Center for Gender Issues and ADHD

3268 Arcadia Place NW, Washington, DC 20015

888-238-8588

www.ncgiadd.org

Organization promoting awareness of, research into, and advocacy for girls and women with ADHD.

- Original, out-of-the-box thinking.
- A tendency to look at life in unusual ways, a zany sense of humor, an unpredictable approach to anything and everything.
- Remarkable persistence and resilience, if not stubbornness.
- Warmhearted and generous behavior.
- Extrasensitive, with accurate gut feelings.

Disadvantageous characteristics:

- Difficulty in turning great ideas into significant actions.
- Difficulty in explaining yourself to others.
- Chronic underachievement. You may be floundering in school, or you may achieve at a high level. Getting good grades or being president of the student council does not rule out the diagnosis of ADD. You know you could be achieving at a higher level if only you could "find the key."
- Mood often angry or down in the dumps due to frustration.
- Major problems in handling money.
- Poor tolerance of frustration.
- Inconsistent performance despite great effort. People with ADD do great one hour and lousy the next, or great one day and lousy the next, regardless of effort and time in preparation.

Common Questions and Answers About ADD
by Edward M. Hallowell, MD

1. **Q.: What is ADD?**

   A.: Attention Deficit Disorder is a name for a collection of symptoms, some positive, some negative. Having ADD is like having a turbo-charged race-car brain. If you take certain specific steps, then you can take advantage of the benefits ADD provides—while avoiding the disasters it can create. Some of our most successful entrepreneurs have ADD, as do some of our most creative actors, writers, doctors, scientists, attorneys, architects, athletes, and dynamic people in all walks of life.

2. **Q.: What are the typical features of a person who has ADD?**

   A.: The core symptoms of ADD are excessive distractibility (hard time focusing), impulsivity (reacting too quickly without thinking), and restlessness (hard time staying still in body and mind). These can lead children to do poorly at school and at play, even when they are bright and try hard.

   In addition, children who have ADD may also have some of the following characteristics:

Advantageous characteristics:

- Many creative talents, usually not fully used until the diagnosis is made.

- History of being labeled "lazy" or "a spaceshot" or an "attitude problem" by teachers or parents who do not understand what is really going on (i.e., having ADD).
- Trouble with organization. Kids with ADD organize by stuffing book bags and closets.
- Trouble with time management. People with ADD are terrible at estimating in advance how long a task will take, putting off homework and long-term assignments and rushing to get things done at the last minute.
- Search for high stimulation. People with ADD often are drawn to danger or excitement in order to focus.
- Tendency to be a maverick, doing things in your own unusual way. (This can be an advantage or a disadvantage!)
- Impatience. People with ADD can't stand waiting in lines or waiting for others to get to the point.
- Chronic wandering of the mind, or what is called distractibility. Tendency to tune out or drift away in the middle of a page or a conversation. Tendency to change subjects abruptly.
- Tendency to self-medicate with alcohol or other drugs, or with addictive activities such as shopping, eating, or risk taking.
- Trouble staying put with one activity until it is done.
- Tendency to change channels, change plans, change direction for no apparent reason.
- Failure to learn from mistakes. People with ADD will often use the same strategy that failed them before.

- Easily forget your own failings and those of others. You are quick to forgive, in part because you are quick to forget.
- Difficulty in reading social cues, which can lead to difficulty in making and keeping friends.
- Tendency to get lost in own thoughts, no matter what else might be going on.

3. Q.: Aren't most people somewhat like this?

A.: The diagnosis of ADD is based not upon the presence of these symptoms—which most people have now and then—but on how intense and how long the symptoms are present. If you have the symptoms intensely, as compared with a group of your peers, and if you have had them all your life, you may have ADD.

4. Q.: What causes ADD? Is it inherited?

A.: We don't know exactly what causes ADD, but we do know it runs in families. We estimate that about 5 percent to 8 percent of a random sample of children have ADD. If one parent has it, the chances of a child's developing it shoot up to about 30 percent; if both parents, the chances leap to over 50 percent. Genetics don't tell the whole story. You can also acquire ADD through lack of oxygen at birth or from a head injury or if your mother drank too much alcohol during pregnancy or from elevated lead levels or perhaps even from food allergies and environmental chemical sensitivities, and in other ways we don't yet understand.

5. Q.: Does ADD ever go away on its own?

A.: Yes. The symptoms of ADD disappear during puberty in from 30 percent to 40 percent of children, and the symptoms stay gone. As the brain matures, it changes in ways that may cause the negative symptoms to disappear. In addition, sometimes teens learn how to compensate so well for their ADD during puberty that it looks as if the ADD has gone away, even if it hasn't.

6. Q.: Is ADD overdiagnosed?

A.: Yes and no. It is overdiagnosed in some places, underdiagnosed in others. There are schools and regions where every child who blinks fast seems to get diagnosed with ADD. At the same time, there are places around the country where doctors refuse to make the diagnosis at all because they "don't believe in ADD." ADD is not a religious principle; it is a medical diagnosis derived from such solid evidence as genetic studies, brain scans, and worldwide epidemiological surveys.

7. Q.: What is the proper procedure to diagnose ADD?

A.: There is no one surefire test. The best way to diagnose ADD is to combine several tests. The most powerful "test" is your own story, which doctors call your history. As you tell your story, your doctor will be listening for how your attention has varied in different settings throughout your life. In the case of ADD, it is important that the history be taken from at least two people in addition to you, per-haps a parent, teacher, coach, grandparent, or babysitter, since people with ADD are often not good at observing themselves.

The best doctors also include a search for talents and strengths, as these are the key to the most successful treat-ments.

8. Q.: Who should I go to see to get a diagnosis?

A.: The best way to find doctors who know what they are doing is to get a referral from someone you know who has had good experiences with those doctors.

The degrees these persons have are much less important than their experience. People from different backgrounds may be capable of helping you. Child psychiatrists have the most training in ADD. Developmental pediatricians (a pedia-trician with some extra training) are also good with ADD, but they are in short supply. Some regular pediatricians are excellent at diagnosing and treating ADD, whereas others—those who have not had much experience with ADD—are understandably less skilled. Some family practitioners and some internists are good. Some psychiatrists who specialize in treating adults do not have training in ADD. However, most psychologists do.

If you cannot get a referral from someone you know, pri-mary care doctors are often very good at making recommen-dations and referrals.

9. Q.: **What other problems should I be on the lookout for?**

A.: Trouble in school or at home. Consistent under-achievement, especially when behavior problems aren't no-ticeable. Sometimes when the ADD is diagnosed and treated, the trouble, whatever it is, or the underachievement goes away. Often tutoring, family therapy, individual therapy, and coaching can help.

10. Q.: **What is the best treatment for ADD?**

A.: It varies. The best approach to treating ADD is to follow a plan specifically designed for you. One size does not fit all. You'll want to talk with your doctor and your parents to find the right strategies for you. If it doesn't work, don't give up. Your plan should always be open to revision.

11. Q.: **What are the most common key ingredients of such a comprehensive plan?**

A.: Keep the following in mind:

1. Diagnosis, as well as identification of talents and strengths
2. Implementation of a five-step plan that promotes tal-ents and strengths (see question number 14 for a de-scription of this)
3. Education about ADD
4. Changes in lifestyle (this might include reducing time spent watching TV and playing electronic games,

increasing time with family and friends, and devoting more time to physical exercise)

5. Development of routines emphasizing organization
6. Counseling of some kind, such as coaching, psychotherapy, or family or individual therapy
7. Following an exercise program that stimulates the cerebellum, targeted tutoring, general physical exercise, occupational therapy, and nutritional supplements such as omega-3 fatty acids (found in fish oil)
8. Medication

12. Q.: How does this comprehensive plan help?

A.: Getting a name for what's been going on usually brings relief. When you get a diagnosis of ADD, you can finally shed all those blaming, shaming "moral" diagnoses, like *lazy*, *weak*, *undisciplined*, or, simply, *bad*.

The identification of talents and strengths is one of the most important parts of the treatment. People with ADD usually know their shortcomings all too well, but their talents and strengths have been overshadowed by what's been going wrong.

13. Q: What is the five-step plan that promotes talents and strengths?

A: The first step is to *connect*—with a teacher, a coach, a mentor, a supervisor, or a friend, and don't forget God or whatever your spiritual life leads you toward. Once you feel connected, you will feel safe enough to go to step 2, which is to *play*. In play, you discover your talents and strengths. Play includes any activity in which your brain lights up and you get imaginatively involved. When you find some form of play you like, you do it over and over again. This is step 3, *practice*. As you practice, you get better; this is step 4, *mastery*. When you achieve mastery, other people notice and give you *recognition*; this is step 5. Recognition, in turn, connects you with the people who recognize and value you, which brings you back to step 1, *connect*, and deepens the connection.

Beware, however, of jumping in at step 3. That's the mistake many parents, teachers, and coaches make: they demand practice and offer recognition as the reward. This may help at first, but can lead to fatigue and burnout in the long run.

For this plan to be effective, it must not be forced on you by others. To do that, you must start with connection and play.

14. Q.: What if you're not good at anything, or what if what you're good at is illegal, dangerous, or simply lacking in any social value, like playing Nintendo?

A.: *Everyone* has the seed of a talent. Everyone has some interest that can be turned into a skill that is legal, reasonably safe, and has value both to that person and to society. *Everyone*. The work of treating ADD is to find that talent or interest. It may be hidden. For example, if what you're good at seems not to have a social value, like playing Nintendo, you might want to eventually get a job at a computer game store or you might want to take a course on designing computer games.

The germ of a great life often lies hidden in the useless activities we love. Look for that germ. If you can't find it, get someone else to help you look.

15. **Q.: What are the most important changes I can make to lead a better life?**
    A: They are as follows:
    Positive human contact. Make sure you get enough smiles, hugs, waves hello, and warm handshakes.
    Reduce electronics (television, video games, the Internet, etc.). Video games, computer games, and the like are not inherently bad or dangerous. In moderation, especially when played in groups, they can help develop social skills, turn taking, and friendships. Too much time spent in front of a screen keeps you from reaching out, making friends, and practicing important life skills that help reduce impulsivity and restlessness. Moderation is the key.
    Sleep. Enough sleep is that amount of sleep that allows you to wake up without an alarm clock.
    Diet. Eat a balanced diet. Eat protein as part of breakfast. Protein is the best long-lasting source of brain fuel. Adding omega-3 fatty acids to the diet is useful for health in general. Fish oil is a great source of omega-3 fatty acids. Because it works as a mood enhancer, fish oil can, in rare instances, trigger manic or depressive episodes in extraordinarily sensitive people with bipolar disorder. So never take fish oil without first telling a physician monitoring your care. Adding antioxidants to

the diet can also help. Grape-seed extract is one of nature's most potent source of antioxidants; so are blueberries.

Exercise. Regular exercise is one of the best gifts you can give your brain. Even if it's just walking for fifteen minutes, exercise every day. Exercising is like taking medication for ADD in a holistic, natural way.

Prayer or meditation. Both of these help calm and focus the mind.

16. Q.: What is coaching and tutoring as it applies to ADD?

A.: An ADD coach is someone, other than a parent, who can help you get organized and stay on track. Coaches are available in many shapes and sizes, from the ultraexpensive executive coaches to the ultrainexpensive grandpa who coaches for free. There are national coaching organizations you can contact online for more information.

For many kids, the most important intervention is tutoring targeted to correct specific problems or symptoms. For example, if you have trouble with writing essays or doing algebra or reading, you should get help specifically aimed at these problems. To learn about finding such a professional, go to www.aetonline.org.

17. Q.: What about medication?

A.: You should never take medication until you know the facts and feel comfortable doing so. When used properly, the medications for ADD are safe and effective. Research shows that medication is the single most effective treatment for ADD. It works for 80 percent to 90 percent of people who try it. When these medications work, they can increase mental focus and reduce impulsivity. The most commonly used medications are stimulants such as Ritalin and Adderal and their long-acting equivalents such as Concerta, Ritalin LA, and Adderal XR. The nonstimulant amantadine has been used to great advantage in treating ADD, as has bupropion (Wellbutrin) and the newest nonstimulant, Strattera. If you are considering taking medication for ADD, be sure to see a doctor who has experience in prescribing it. Even small dose changes can make a big difference.

18. **Q.: What else should I know about stimulant medications?**

   A.: Here are some quick facts about stimulants, or STs:

   - STs take effect in about twenty minutes and last from four to twelve hours, depending on which one is taken.
   - You may stop and start STs at will. For example, you can stop taking them over the summer or on weekends. Unlike antibiotics or antidepressants, you do not need to maintain a steady blood level of STs to benefit. When you stop the STs, you lose the benefit until you start them up again.
   - If you start on STs and get some benefit, that does not mean you will need to take STs for the rest of your life.

Sometimes these new habits you learn while taking STs carry over to when you aren't taking them, allowing you to discontinue the STs.

- There are no *known* dangers associated with long-term use of STs. The side effects that are going to show up usually occur right away.

- STs are not addicting or habit forming if taken properly. On the other hand, if you grind them up and snort them or inject them, as some people do, then they are dangerous.

- STs do not lead to the abuse of illicit drugs. To the contrary, studies show that taking STs reduces the likelihood that you will take illegal drugs.

- STs or some other nonstimulant medication like Strattera or Wellbutrin will work (i.e., improve mental focus without producing side effects that warrant stopping the medication) 80 percent to 90 percent of the time in people who have ADD. That means that 10 percent to 20 percent of the time, no medication will help.

- No one should ever be compelled to take STs or any other medication for ADD. This creates struggles that lead to bad outcomes.